26.2 MILES TO HAPPINESS

26.2 MILES TO HAPPINESS

A Comedian's Tale of Running, Red Wine and Redemption

PAUL TONKINSON

BLOOMSBURY SPORT

LONDON • OXFORD • NEW YORK • NEW DELHI • SYDNEY

BLOOMSBURY SPORT
Bloomsbury Publishing Plc
50 Bedford Square London WC1B 3DP UK

BLOOMSBURY, BLOOMSBURY SPORT and the Diana logo are trademarks
of Bloomsbury Publishing Plc

First published in Great Britain 2020

ISBN: HB: 978-1-4729-6626-1; eBook: 978-1-4729-6627-8

2 4 6 8 10 9 7 5 3 1

Typeset in ITC Century by Deanta Global Publishing Services, Chennai, India
Printed and bound in Great Britain by CPI Group (UK) Ltd. Croydon, CRO 4YY

To find out more about our authors and books visit www.bloomsbury.com
and sign up for our newsletters

To Ra

RENFREWSHIRE COUNCIL	
249903521	
Bertrams	28/01/2020
796.425	£14.99
RAL	

Contents

Preface

The dawning of the New Year saw a plan percolating in my mind. A faint notion that possibly, just possibly, this could be the year I would run a marathon in under three hours and write a book about it.

The last few years had seen me running more and more. I'd also been doing a lot of writing, thinking and talking about running, both in my column for *Runner's World* and on the podcast Running Commentary. I'd joined a club and had found much fun and inspiration within the running community. I was feeling grateful and wanted, as they say, to give something back.

There are a great many running books around, often inspirational tomes detailing epic adventures, which I've devoured hungrily. I noticed a pattern had emerged within their pages, almost a formula mapping the startlingly transformative qualities of the running life: the author as protagonist changed beyond all comprehension. These books, which I love and constantly return to, would typically start off in the middle of an epic adventure...

It's Mile 45 in the Cross Antarctic Ultra Midnight Challenge. The temperature's –5, with a wind chill of –17. I've been running continuously for 37 hours and I can't feel my face, legs or feet. In fact, I should say leg – I've just sawn my lower right limb off and am licking it feverishly for nutrition. Having long since broken through all the notions of normal human behaviour, I am soothed by the taste of my own flesh. Breath freezes and shatters in front of me with every step across the lunar icy floor, it dissolves in front of my eyes, blending into the thousands of stars above me, which festoon the jet-black sky... I am lost and, due to extreme fatigue, vision is fading fast. Is that a bear in front of me? It's hard to say; I am suddenly rendered blind. I hear a blood-curdling roar, my nostrils are seared by hot bear breath. I turn and run, as best I can, blind, on one leg through the snow. Will I live? Will I die? As my one remaining foot smashes through a sheet of ice into the freezing waters below, a barbaric yawp escapes me up and away into the cold, unforgiving Arctic night.

Suddenly swallowed by a gigantic shadow I dimly sense the bear approaching, it's like the eclipse of my soul. My frozen hands desperately claw at the ice like clumps of dead meat.

Is this my final moment?

For a second, I ponder: *How did I get here?*

Cut to: Two years earlier.

If ever there was a more unlikely runner, I've yet to meet one. As an overweight, chain-smoking, meat-ingesting alcoholic, the only running I ever did was to the burger stall at half-time. More of a waddle, really.

This gently parody is not delivered to deny the power of these epic journeys. I love these books and thrill to the stories. The truth is, I couldn't even attempt to tread on the same turf, never mind compete. For me, there was no real before and after. I'd always loved running, even as a child. If I see a space, I imagine myself running through it; that's just how I see the world.

My effort was to be a humbler affair, a fairly simple detailing of my attempts to run a marathon in under three hours, intended for the fun runner and serious runner alike. I have been both and, in fact, see no difference. Rather unusually for me, the notion became a reality – the book you're currently holding.

At its simplest level, this book wants to persuade you to run a marathon. If you've already done one, it wants you to run another and really commit to your best effort. I truly believe running a marathon is an experience everyone should have once in a lifetime, existing as it does on that perfect parabola of difficulty and attainability. It's tough but doable, and the journey to get there is richer than you'd imagine.

As I settled at my table and tentatively launched forth, the writing of the book began to mirror the act of running a marathon itself. There were stages where I felt carried aloft by angels and others where I felt despair, wondering whether I'd finish it. Gradually the training and the writing started to fuse; I was giving myself wholeheartedly to both.

The end result surprised me. This was not the book I set out to write. It details a few months in the spring of 2017 when I allowed my extremist nature to run wild and gave myself fully and simply to a very simple task – running a marathon as quickly as possible.

Like all of us – and to paraphrase Walt Whitman – I am large, I contain multitudes; so the book is both serious and funny. It combines some very practical advice with the odd flight of philosophical fancy, for which I hope you'll forgive me. There are nuggets of showbiz, but it also contains some deeply personal moments – moments that emerged in the writing unplanned, revealing themselves while I explored this mysterious beast.

That's all I can say at this juncture.

Like a Zen master pointing to the moon, the only way of explaining the marathon is to point to the marathon itself, the actual event, the experience of which is different for every one of us. Reading about running is great, but it is only through the running of a marathon that you will understand it. Once you emerge blinking into the light, rinsed and broken by the Wall, but unbowed – only then will you see it.

There's a saying in stand-up comedy, a joke really, which acts often finish on. They say if you can make just one person laugh onstage, you've had a terrible gig. Well, this book's different. If I can nudge just one person to run a marathon, my work here is done.

I hope the book surprises you.

5.45 a.m. Race Day

'The start is a wonderful moment. For a fleeting moment, it is as if mankind is joined together, we are totally one, facing the same direction.'

Jean Christophe (Frenchman, flâneur, friend)

I've slept.

That's my first thought upon waking, and a blessed relief. The good stuff as well: deeply restorative, miraculous, refreshing sleep. Thank goodness. It can be hard the night before. Excitement's off the scale; think Christmas as a six-year-old. Marathon Eve can send you tossing and turning for hours. The knowledge that to prepare for the energy-sapping lunacy of a marathon you need to rest can easily scupper your plans. In years gone by, there'd been late nights. I'd even thrown gigs into the mix: Comedy Store late shows in London's Leicester Square; zigzagging across town till 2 a.m. like a clown (literally) as a prelude to a few hours of sweaty, adrenalised, spiralling panic. That year, marathon morning's alarm had slowly insinuated itself into a much delayed but profoundly deep reverie, wrenched me from heaven, crashed into my REMs with a panicky poke, and said, *Grab your kit, you tit, you're late!* Late – on marathon morning. The sheer stupidity of it. Instead of a leisurely morning, I was trapped in an anxiety dream of my own creation. Late. *Jump in a cab, step on it* late. *Circumnavigating the security cordon of the marathon in confused panic* late. *Jumping out running to the start to run from the start* late. Raiding the larder already for stores of mental and physical energy that I did not possess. Already knackered for a marathon that I'd not really trained for and, all in all, undisputed winner of London Marathon's Most Idiotic Man of the Year Award.

I have learned my lesson. This year was different; an aura of deep peace settled upon the valley. I'd done it right this time: no gigs the night before; in fact, no gigs the previous three nights. Some would say, given my current financial situation, this is a tad overcommitted. Still, I'm rested. OK, the kids are sporting a slightly undernourished, haunted look, Netflix is down and there are red letters through the postbox – but Dad's *ready for the marathon*.

I've followed the programme, done the miles, stuffed the carbs, visualised, stretched, been massaged, pummelled. I am peaking.

The evening before the marathon, we scoffed the last remnants of papa's bolognese with a ceremonial gravity. All was quiet at Tonkinson Towers. Family rituals had shifted to accommodate the following day's battle. Ra, my glorious wife, had made the ultimate sacrifice of a no-wine Saturday. Teenage kids had desisted from inviting any mates back to their 'yard' (the family kitchen) for preloading, a mysterious ritual involving the drinking of much booze and the sequestering of more booze upon their person to sneak into establishments that served booze in order to drink their own. Even the dogs seemed calmer; the two wire-haired dachshunds (the jet-black Dashy and sandy blonde Calypso) had snuffled down early doors, licking my Achilles tendon in a wonderfully intuitive canine gesture of solidarity, as if in anticipation of the carnage that the morrow would bring.

In my bedroom as I prepared to snuggle down on freshly laundered sheets, I perused my training diaries from the last few months with gleeful serenity. They say the map is not the territory, and it's true: the scribbled digits and brief descriptions only hinted at the huge ups and downs that had occurred in the last few months. The journey both physically and mentally had been tumultuous, but the diaries did undeniably point to loads of running – and, as running was what I was planning on doing the following day, I seemed well set. Placing my marathon kit at the end of the bed like a Christmas stocking, my head took the long fall onto the sweet cushions and I swiftly succumbed to the oceanic slumber of the innocent.

5.45 a.m. The first few seconds of peace upon waking are swiftly scrubbed by the sharp reset of a new morning. Today is marathon day. Yikes. The internal monologue quickly kicks in. *This is it. I've done the work. Time to cash in your chips. You've got this. Do it. Run hard. Relax. Feel free to think in longer sentences.* It's like being trapped in a Tony Robbins seminar. The truth is, I'm incredibly hyped; I don't think I've ever felt as determined in my life. Maybe as a kid for school cross-country or a brief skirmish with Sunday league football on Hackney Marshes in my mid-30s. Those keyed me in, briefly, to an ultra-competitive state that I'd long since abandoned. It's good to be back, and I know enough about myself now to keep a lid on my rampant anxiety.

Rituals have been established:

6.00 a.m. Breakfast, water, coffee. Absolutely essential. Not much is needed, I've been filling up with carbohydrates in a slightly demented fashion the last few days, so it's a couple of slices of malt loaf, half a banana. Really, it's just a top-up to *get the system going.*

6.25 a.m. Checking the bag. Primarily the three absolute essentials: vest, shorts, trainers. Now, this moment can get a bit fetishistic. From a distance it might look like I'm caressing, kissing the race trainers. Maybe. There's certainly a sacramental nature to the movement as I place the kit on the bed before me, and I for one would never judge any action you deem appropriate at this stage of race prep. For me personally, at that very second when I peruse the race kit, it's probably a feeling akin to love. These are, after all, the accoutrements of battle, they will carry me forth. Behold the majesty of the London Heathside club vest with its royal blue hue bordered by a fiery blade of red and yellow. Witness the glory of the black Ron Hill marathon shorts, borderline obscenely skimpy, definitely unsuitable for anything but an athletic context and certain parties underneath the arches in Vauxhall. Don't pay much attention to the ultra-thin marathon socks, but feel free to genuflect and marvel at the altar of the recently purchased new release Adidas Boston race shoes, a snip at £95(!).

Other items fill out the regulation London Marathon plastic bag. Sports drink for last-minute, pre-race replenishment. A banana, because, well, what situation isn't improved by a banana? GU gels. (Gels could have a chapter all to themselves. Today, I'm doing, for the first time, a gel every 40 minutes, alternating espresso and caramel sachets; other flavours are available.) I've also packed a towel, a T-shirt for post-race warmth and, of course, a bottle of water. (Everyone should have a bottle of water on them at all times. Check now if you haven't got one, notify the authorities immediately and make your way to a place of safety.) Then the medical stuff: plasters for nipples, Vaseline for armpits and Baby Bottom Butter for ... shall we say the smoothing of the undercarriage? Those testicles aren't going to look after themselves, you know! Not to be indelicate while being indelicate, the plasters, Vaseline and Bottom Butter are a must. After my first marathon, the photo at the finish line looked like an outtake from *Platoon*, two rivulets of blood streaming down my chest. I was running as if my pants were on fire, which is exactly how it felt.

6.50 a.m. Departure. Ra drops me at Finsbury Park and I'm off then, alone. The next time I see her will be at the finish. Rudy, my youngest at 14, will be there as well; the other two – George, 18, and Bonnie, 17 – have reached the age where waiting for two hours on The Mall for Dad to finish on a Sunday is 'dead'. All I can say is I'm incredibly glad little Rudy's going with his mum; I'll be thinking of him as I run.

The great thing about setting off is that it starts the countdown, three hours till the race starts. In jumping on the Tube I join a tribe of runners gradually assembling. I spot them peppered throughout the Tube coming down from Finsbury. They are stretching, yawning nervously, checking Fitbits, surreptitiously feeling for a pulse on their wrist. Smiles ricochet around the carriage. The air fizzes with anticipation. Fancy-dress outfits slowly infiltrate the Metropolitan Line. At Bank, a man dressed as a banana and wearing Asics trainers hops on board; opposite him, a man holding a pantomime horse's head is doing the *Telegraph* crossword. The ratio of runners to non-runners is around 50:50 as I stop off at Monument. I'm meeting my running mate Rob Deering to record a marathon special podcast pre-race. It's nice to hop off the Tube for a second. I pop in to a Pret A Manger, it's awash with runners of all shapes and sizes. The queue for the toilets is four deep. People avoid each other's gaze, fidgeting while they stand. Tension accumulates as the start gets closer. People react in different ways; some babble excitedly, others seem sullen and retreat into headphones. The train on the way to Maze Hill is crammed with marathon types. Stray civilians stand trapped, encircled by the rising babble of maranoia: injury woes, pacing issues, gel confusion. Sitting across from us is a very chatty Scottish man in full chain body armour. Dave is from Arboath. He's red-faced already and cackling like a lunatic. *Why are you doing it?* comes the obvious question.

'Why not?' he retorts.

Looking at him, I can't imagine the day that lies in store. To run a marathon is ridiculously hard, to run in full chain body armour seems ludicrous. Has he run one before?

'Aye. It's my fifth,' he fires back. 'Nae botha!' There's not an inch of fat on the parts of his body that are visible to the naked eye (his face and upper neck) and his eyes sparkle with giddy self-awareness; he knows he's a bit odd. 'I know it sounds daft, I just really enjoy it, you know. I run it with mates from school. It's like a reunion.'

He rises to say his goodbyes. 'Any road, I'm away to the blue start to meet them and pick up the cannon.'

Cannon?

'You need a cannon if you're going to war,' he says matter of factly, as if telling a child not to touch the oven. With that he puts on his helmet, pulls up his visor and disappears into the melee.

A stream of runners spills out at Maze Hill station. Something huge is happening in Greenwich, an army is gathering. Men and women of all ages, genders, nationalities and ability. Club runners, first-timers, veterans, the obviously fit and the obviously fat. Rob and I make our way to the Green start. We mike up to record our observations. It's incredible to be part of this teeming river of humanity, this rolling carnival of marathon mayhem. Flags unfurl, banners fly, more fancy dress. I notice a lot of vegetables this year. Within two minutes I spy an aubergine, two tomatoes and a man who is, I think, a courgette; it's basically an allotment in human form. We chat to Wonder Woman, who's down from Stoke and aiming for a sub-4 marathon. Across the road, Rob spots a moody Father Christmas urinating against a fence. Many people have names written on their tops and photos – tributes. The fact that so many people are running to honour loved ones suffuses the whole day with an emotional undercurrent. It gives it a depth amid the almost medieval gaiety.

Volunteers cheerfully point us in the right direction. There's plenty of time, but the volume of people is immense, thousands upon thousands. I'm trying to keep focused, and rein in my excitement, but it's impossible to contain, the collective energy is infectious, intoxicating. Our bodies are coiled like springs. We've trained for months, tapered up, now we're ready to go, straining at the leash.

The mass Green start sprawls out over the Greenwich common. Club flags have popped up, charity groups cluster. There are tents, coffee bars, massage areas, container lorries for kit – and people; loads of people. Nerves are fraying slightly, smiles seem a tad nervous, eye contact is haphazard. Mania nibbles at the edges of everyday chat. It's all well and good, we all know we're at the start of a great and momentous day, but it's not started yet. We're in the *too early to get really nervous, but this is nowhere near normal* zone. There are six queues for the portaloos and each one snakes a good quarter mile across the common.

The weather is perfect: overcast, coolish with absolutely no breeze. We cut across the common to the celebrity tent. Our names are on the list. We're in. There, inside the tent, if it's possible, the tension cranks up a notch.

A light giddiness prevails, the frequency has changed. PAs flitter twixt the stars, the air reverberates with the clicking of cameras. Famous people like seeing other famous people, and non-famous people like me like watching famous people mingle. And we're all in a tent, which isn't that big.

The usual suspects are evident: Chris Evans, Sophie Raworth, Danny Mills, James Cracknell, Mark Chapman, assorted DJs, soap stars, actors, charity award winners. Many fall under the category of people *I know the look of but have no idea who they are* – the same category of which I am a proud member. Indeed, it's fair to say my celebrity status is confusing to myself as well as others. I place myself firmly in the chancer category, I'm under no illusions. Still, I'm more than ready to milk it; it means you get away cleanly at the start, the toilets are accessible and the food's great.

A long table at the far end overflows with a cascade of pre -marathon goodies: mini Mars bars, bananas, grapes, flapjacks, biscuits, muffins, bacon rolls – what kind of fool eats a bacon roll an hour before the marathon?

Hailing from the North, I'm of an almost aggressively friendly persuasion and, as a compulsive chatterer, I'm in heaven. Folk I wouldn't normally be able to get my teeth into are actually in front of me; it's like Twitter, but real. I grab a coffee and scan, sniper-like, looking for an opening. Faces removed from their natural setting slowly come into focus and then, *yes, I see... Is it..? It is* ex Manchester Utd midfielder Quinton Fortune. I love football and by extension footballers, so any chance, I'm at it. There's absolutely no rational reason for me to do so, he's standing at the edge of the tent, but I casually mosey over, feigning interest in a table top. I keep a dignified distance for a moment before, having secured what looks like a nod from the woman next to him who might be his PA, I plunge into his personal space. He was a hard player and like many hard players, a very sweet man. Of course, being footballers, I reason that all anyone wants to talk to them about is football, so I make a point of talking about anything but football, despite the fact that's all I want to talk about and all they want to as well. We settle on the marathon; the onset of extreme physical pain is very bonding. It's Quinton's first London marathon, so we talk training, times; I always deeply envy first-time Londoners. I genuinely believe that they are on the cusp of a life-changing event. I can quickly get borderline messianic rhapsodising about the experience that awaits, and it's not long before I clock that I'm being way too intense with poor Quinton. At moments like this, I realise that I am not a cool person; it's like I've never been out. There's a pause in conversation as our body language shifts. Quinton's PA hovers; whatever has been happening has reached its natural conclusion. I'm terrible at chat extrication, so try to stand jauntily at a slighter more obtuse angle, my body language saying I'm open to the room – or more accurately, I'm drifting off into the abyss, when suddenly a life raft, in the form of a hand, sticks out.

'Hi, Paul. Vassos. Alexander.'

As if I could forget! Vassos Alexander. Running author and legend – and Chris Evans' sidekick on his breakfast show (first for Radio 2, now Virgin). I grab the hand, a movement that releases Quinton, who makes a quick bolt for freedom. I love Vassos, very friendly fella, he'd done our podcast a few months previously; we'd nipped down to his house in Barnes for a swift 6 miler through lovely parkland accompanied by his Labrador, Holly. He's the kind of runner whose natural training pace is a bit of a stretch for the likes of me; he really is a very fit man and runs like a berserker, long bouncing strides devouring the ground with an intense, infectious abandon. This morning's marathon is, it appears, not his priority, he's training for an ultra – but Vassos being Vassos, not just any ultra. It's the Spartathlon, 153 miles. A soul-grinding yomp from Athens to Sparti on the site of ancient Sparta. That's right, 153 miles without stopping, through the day and night. It's a race with a very high dropout rate, recognised as perhaps the hardest foot race on the planet. The ultimate test. If anyone can do it, old Vassos can. His eyes shine talking about the course, he radiates a puppyish sense of fun – but that's one tough Greek, there's no mistaking it. He looks fresh after a 19-mile (30km) hill session the previous day, the logic being that it will stop him running too fast today. It's at moments like this that I see very clearly I'm surrounded by maniacs.

The range of abilities in celeb world is wide. James Cracknell's very fast; his marathon pb is an extremely nippy 02:43:12 and he carries himself with the focus and crazed bonhomie of an ex-Olympian. Raworth's ultra keen, constantly improving, very focused. If I had to put money on it, I'd wager she was head girl back in the day. She's the type of character who'd thrash you at interhouse hockey and then beat you to the showers, combining a real sense of fun with an overwhelming impression of capability, utter fearlessness. It's very impressive. She follows a strict training schedule, has her own personal pacer for the day and is aiming for sub 03:30:00, which I imagine she'll get.

Pre-race routines take hold. Mostly, at this stage, of a practical nature. Numbers are pinned to vests (a fidgety process best done early), race socks donned, trainers put on. Other celebs saunter into range. *EastEnders* Hall of Famer Ian Beale emerges blinking into the light, a character indelibly scorched into my mind as the poor fella stood up by Michelle on his wedding day all those years ago. He confesses to being a tad hungover and is scoffing a bacon sarnie (d'oh!). I spare him the Fortune treatment, keeping the conversation light. What a lovely humble man he is, bigger in real life. Not the pushover of the Square. The size thing seems to be a theme; maybe I'm projecting. Chris Evans seems massive, there'll be no chat with him, way too big in every respect. He strides round the tent like a nobleman in *Game of Thrones*. At any moment I expect him to corral a couple of dragons together and invade the eastern territories.

I snaggle a few words with Mark Chapman, yet another stupendously large human. (What's happening? Is it nerves? Am I physically shrinking?) Now, I love Chappers, his breadth of knowledge about sport is amazing and he's superb in every area, with amazing fact-retention. I'd sort of planned on telling him this, in particular congratulating him on his expert anchoring of the Monday night American football show on BBC, and so, when given the opportunity, I do, blasting him with fulsome praise from both barrels.

Chapman bears my onslaught with good grace. His eyes seem to glaze over a couple of times, then I realise it's just toilet queue tension.

Back in the tent and immediately engulfed in a swift embrace from author and all-round force of nature Bryony Gordon. She's never run a marathon before and is ricocheting around the tent with her irresistible joie de vivre.

'Tell me, Paul, is it going to hurt?'

'Yes.' (Why lie?) 'It's going to hurt. But, you've done the training, haven't you?'

'Oh, I've done it all,' she blusters. 'I'm surprised there's any training left. It's a miracle to me you can even say the word.'

Bryony's a natural wit, a great person to have around. She's so open with her panic it renders any panic you may be personally feeling meaningless.

30 minutes to the start. Preparation ramps up. Nuts and bolts stuff, plasters on nipples, the greasing of parts, absolutely essential business. This can be done in conversation, but I choose to keep my dignity and turn my back as I plaster up. There's a not-so-subtle moob situation that I have no desire to inflict on the population at large; Marathon Day is tough enough as it is. It's odd, I've trained like a dog for this, I'm fitter than I've ever been in my life, but at certain angles – getting out of the bath, for instance – I'm a walking advertisement for a sports bra. The aroma of Vaseline permeates the tent, mixing with the fresh coffee and croissants. Again, this can be administered privately or in company. Being a sensitive soul, I grease my inner thigh and armpits with discretion. Others are less coy. Cracknell is, to be honest, a bit of a beast, a feral God among men. He works his groin with Vaseline like he's starting a lawnmower. If he were to do it in a normal scenario, I reckon he'd be immediately arrested. Different rules apply here. We know that. It's about the race. All this celeb chitchat is all well and good, but we know what's going to happen and in 17 miles' time nobody's going to care about social niceties in the tent. If it's a toss-up between an uncomfortable moment here or dry thighs there, we will not be standing on ceremony. Even so, I gaze in open-eyed wonder 10 minutes later, when the Baby Bottom Butter comes out and a young gentleman, I think he's a rugby player, shamelessly applies it to his testicles mid-conversation with broadcaster Jenni Falconer.

20 minutes to the start. Noise levels seem to rise suddenly as the tent surges with an animalistic urgency. Everyone's doing everything faster. Draining coffee cups, dropping bags off in the lorries. We're ready to go, kits on, just a T-shirt to be discarded before the start. No point drinking any more. Realisation seems to dawn at this point, we're here to run a marathon. It's good to have Deering here; we stretch gently and giggle at the vaguely hysterical atmosphere. Beale looks like the bacon roll is repeating on him. Cracknell's got this strange, thousand-mile stare going on. Raworth chatters away ten to the dozen. Bryony Gordon lollops round the tent not really knowing where to put herself.

I'm breathing deeply, trying to stay calm. I've visualised all this before: the arriving at the tent, the half an hour before the race, the stretching. I'm in a movie of my own making. The foreground of the morning has been a tad manic, but the background, the zoom-out has been beatific. I feel very secure, cocooned by my preparation for once. I'm in the zone, excited, serene and ferociously determined all at once.

'5 minutes!' comes the cry. We need to be making our way to the start. A very, very last-minute and final, without any doubt, toilet trip. Then, a quick dash/scamper out of the tent and left to the start. I can't quite believe it, it's happening.

I glance right, down onto the dizzyingly large number of runners billowing back out along the road to South London. It's impossible at moments like this not to marvel at the sheer numbers, the incredible popularity of the marathon. It's marathon season. Boston was two weeks ago, Tokyo's in March, Paris is popular this time of year. In the autumn, there's Chicago, New York, Berlin. That's just the big city majors, the big seven. Then add all the other ones, the small town races dotted round the world, trail marathons, exotic locations. The Antarctic, for flippin' sake! Every weekend of the year, all over the world, people are making the bizarre decision to run 26.2 miles. And the spectators, the crowds are making the equally bizarre decision to watch them. Hundreds of thousands of people gathering to scream and cajole, to offer sweets and drinks, to massage our cramping muscles and drag us to the finish. Even before the event, there's the Expo – the three-day commercial extravaganza that has sprung up, an absurdly excessive neurotic festival of advice and gear and diet and seminars, all part of the media machinery that is the modern-day, big-city marathon. There are previews and interviews, Twitter feeds, Facebook pages, analysis serving a global audience watching on screens round the world, shaking off their hangovers to slump on the sofa, switch on the television and watch this explosion of energy in bemused wonderment.

There's the organisation, the closing of the roads, the manning of the drinks stations, the marshals, the clean-up. It's a monster, an ever-growing, multi-tendrilled, energy-ball-chomping brute.

And five months later, it will start again as entry reopens. Every year more people enter. Every year more people finish in this ever-growing phenomenon.

Did Pheidippedes know what he was starting when he set off all those years ago from Marathon to Athens with news of victory? I ran in the '80s during the first running boom; I remember seeing the finish for the first London marathon; running was popular then but still a bit fringe; you'd get shouted at in the street. This is different. Running is mainstream. Everybody's jumped in. London streets have been swarming this spring, the parks peopled with hardy souls at all hours. And now we're here packing in to the start.

3 minutes! I'm right at the back of the front, a few rows off the start line, looking for a club mate who I've arranged to run the first few miles with. Hoggy. We'd made an appointment to find each other 'somewhere near the green start'. A ludicrous suggestion, really, like those plans to hook up with mates by the drum and bass tent sometime during a festival. Yeah, right. Still, I love Hoggy, I've been chasing him round the track all winter, a bond has formed. So I scan the multitude behind me. Hoggy? Is there a Hoggy? Suddenly a voice pipes up from the herd and then, incredibly, he's there, jumping in the air like a thin slither of grinning Scottish salmon. It's a magical moment. We shake hands. He's in the mass start, just a whisper behind, separated from the celebs by a flimsy green ribbon. At the gun I'll drift down the left-hand side of the road and we'll run and chat together.

1 minute to go. T-shirt off, discarded, a quick hug with Deering and then we're jogging on the spot. It's very strange, the moment just before the klaxon starts to set everyone off. A deep hush descends, a silence swelling through the field. Everything is about to change. At this moment we are not running, but in a second we will be: reality will shift. It's an absolutely different state, and very hard to identify with while standing there. Something is approaching: an event, the race, 26.2 miles with all they will contain. The start is imminent; after that we will be on our own. It's what we've all trained for; given everything in training so we can give it everything this morning. Every last one of us. Raworth. Cracknell. Fortune. Hoggy. Deering. Dave from Arbroath, Father Christmas, Wonder Woman, all the vegetables – and 45,000 others. Jean Christophe, my gentle running companion of years past, the man I quoted earlier, who, sadly, can no longer run, is right. It *is* a beautiful moment; for a second we *are* all together, facing the same direction. There is a happiness here, a pure childlike joy in the absurdity of the undertaking. We know we are about to set forth on a path that leads to a body-engulfing pain – and yet, look at us! We seem to be grinning and laughing, crouching, ready to throw ourselves forward like lemmings; our muscles poised, united in a totally singular common purpose.

We're running a marathon. Very soon, the start will split us asunder so we enjoy the last few seconds in company: hands are shaken, good lucks exchanged. Bon voyage!

And yet, for a microsecond as I lean, fingers poised over the watch to set my time as I burst into a new adventure, questions worry at my mind, work their way free and float merrily above the madness of the crowd:

What are we smiling for?
Why are we so happy when we're on the cusp of agony?
What exactly are we playing at?

PART 1

Beginning:
Miles 1-13

1

November. Five months before the marathon. A conversation with Richard

'Well, it's a cry for help, obviously. It's not rocket science. You were denied attention as a child, this is how you react.'

'Nonsense, I enjoy it.'

'Listen, it's a free country and I can't stop you, but please, for the love of God, spare us the never-ending Facebook updates on how your training's going. I may well sponsor you out of loyalty, but I'll be honest, I resent the emotional blackmail. What's more, I don't admire you. In fact, I feel pity more than anything.'

'Can I take this moment to thank you for your continuing support?'

My wife Ra's (Rachel's) 50th was limping towards a messy conclusion. The evening had been a roaring success. Speeches delivered and received with gusto. The dancing and joy had been unconfined in a rented disco floor and bar area full of best mates. We were the rave generation in middle age, dusting down the old tunes, revisiting the old moves, loads of anarchic, sweaty, joyous fun. Problem was, we couldn't just leave it there, there wasn't an early leaver among us. Why couldn't we just reach the end of an evening like normal people and go home at the end of the party? Truth is, our intense hedonistic habits were now ingrained, our definition of a good night forever skewered by the ridiculous and unrepeatable excesses of yesteryear. So when we got together now, oh so rarely, it was a mutual relapse. We didn't party with one eye on the future, we honoured the night, plundering her for all she was worth. After the lights went up and weary bouncers half our age shepherded us onto the street, urging us despairingly to go home, a whispering, lurching, conspiratorial throng formed. The idea of *afters* reared its ugly head; more importantly, the location. Inevitably, we locked arms and waltzed off back to ours.

So, I was lumbered. Time to strap in.

Marathon training and parties don't go that harmoniously. The marathon was months away but I'd been good, a few drinks only. If anything, this made it trickier. Despite the average age of the assembled being over 50, stimulants abounded in various guises; the air buzzed with herbal remedies, a discreet proliferation of powders and tablets leading to an unnatural rigour in the conversation at such a late hour. Even so, energy was ebbing away as morning approached. This would need commitment; more powder would do the trick. Party fiends ransacked the kitchen for booze; it would be a long few hours watching this play out. There was no fighting it, the noise wouldn't let me sleep anyway, so I perched in the corner of the kitchen unobtrusively, slyly placing saucers for ashtrays, providing glasses for confused partygoers as conversations circled and repeated. We'd been here many times, and although I wasn't fully signed up to a night of hedonistic abandon, I loved them all. God knows I'd been an eager participant back in the day.

Over the years, patterns had been established. Exclamations of mutual affection would become more determined over the next few hours. This would merge into dancing. The local 24-hour off-licence would be visited. People who'd stopped smoking would start again. Hands would once more be held aloft, anthems reclaimed. In time, some would fall silent, ease to the edge of the kitchen and hail Ubers. By the end a hard core of revellers, mostly women, but with the odd male intruder, would have chiselled themselves

4

into the form of a deranged rugby scrum careering wildly round the middle of the kitchen to Take That. Husbands would loiter at the periphery of the scrum hoping to remove their wives from its embrace, but the scrum is resilient and would tighten further, providing mutual support to its members, pierced only by the odd glass of wine or trip to the toilet. The men would be awestruck at the stamina of the women in the scrum, the deep thirst for what they call up north *a do*. These were capable professional women; mothers all, as well as TV execs, psychotherapists, teachers, web designers. At some point the scrum, gathering internal velocity and momentum, would veer out into the garden, smashing glasses in its wake before, like scrums eventually always do, collapsing in a mass of bodies. At this point the husbands would saunter onto the field of play and grab their partner. Age would suddenly leap on tired frames, smothering any residual party ideas with the irresistible realisation: time to stop.

Hedonism's wild loud pulse had been chased for the last eight hours; now its opposite would be embraced. Rest and recuperation. Beds would hurriedly avail themselves, sofas nabbed. Party animals would transform in seconds to the meekest of kittens struggling with contact lenses, cleansing rituals instinctively performed, night creams administered, ear plugs inserted.

Then, mercifully, sleep.

All that was yet to come. Before that, though, my old friend Richard had fixed on the marathon as a subject, gained purchase and was getting stuck in.

'You can't actually enjoy it. Don't say that. You don't, and I don't believe you,' he announced.

We were in the kitchen, at 2.25 a.m., the hour of truth. He was sweating furiously, his nasal Weston-super-Mare twang lancing through the Ministry of Sound House Classics compilation playing on the iPod, the primitive reds and blues of the lighting deck dancing up his forehead.

'Honestly, I do. I enjoy it. There's just something in it. It's an amazing day.'

'So's bloody Alton Towers, but you haven't been there seven times!'

His hand quivered slightly as he quaffed the dregs of a fine claret that had been hiding in the corner. I was on the water by now, coming down the hill that he was still definitely cresting. A brief toilet trip five minutes previously had intensified his stake in the discussion. I reckoned if I could weather the next 15 minutes or so, he might just drop it, but for now, he had his teeth in like a hound. Alton Towers was a good point, though; I'd done six marathons, this was my seventh. It was strange, other distances exist, but the marathon kept dragging me back.

'There's something about the distance,' I offered. 'It's got a magic about it.'

'You're right. Agonising blisters, muscle cramp, bleeding nipples.' He lifted his glass emphatically to his lips, 'Great trick.'

Why did I keep doing marathons? What was it?

People run for all sorts of reasons, of course. Lose weight. Get fit. Feel better mentally. Show off. Get a medal. Make friends. Raise money for charity. But you can do that with 10k, a half marathon. What's with the 26.2 miles? It's an extraordinary thing to do. As Richard pointed out, this would be my seventh, and I don't know why, but I wanted to get this one right. I wanted to fully understand it and experience it in a way I'd never done before. The whole thing felt very powerful.

'There are magical elements to it,' I parried. 'The truth is, it changes you. Every marathon shifts the way you relate to the world slightly.'

'It does if you end up limping to the Tube wrapped in a bin bag.'

'You're not getting it. The truth is, you haven't done one. How can you understand it?'

That stung him a bit. Friendship leads to shared history, which leads to knowledge that can be ever so slightly weaponised. I knew part of him wanted to be fitter, though he had never to my knowledge run a step in his life; I'd only ever seen him change pace at zebra crossings. He's a very intelligent man, though, and no fool; his riposte came in measured tones.

'You're right. I haven't run a marathon. But I have actually done some research. I've talked to many a runner, lots of marathon runners, and I've reached a chilling, undeniable conclusion.'

'Oh, I'm sensing it's coming.'

'It is coming. Do you want to hear my undeniable conclusion?'

'But what if I deny it?'

'You can't,' he countered, mock seriously. 'It's an undeniable conclusion.'

'Which is?'

'All marathon runners are depressed and running away from pain.'

'Wow!'

The kitchen lights seemed to shine a bit too bright at that point. This felt a tad confrontational. I was on the ropes, not out, but stunned certainly. 'That's ridiculous.'

'Is it?'

'You're seriously suggesting all marathon runners are running away from pain?'

'Yes. That's what I'm *seriously* suggesting.' He peered in, grotesquely close to my face. 'Every last one of them.'

And with that, he retreated stealthily to the middle of the kitchen, in a surprisingly smooth version of Michael Jackson's moonwalk, twisted flamboyantly on his heels and was quickly swallowed by the scrum forming in the centre of the kitchen.

2

Scarborough 1981.
The first run

Truth is, I've been running for as long as I can remember.

The last couple of years of primary school showed me that, as the distances got further, I got better. Nothing freakish; local press weren't informed of this sensation they had up at Wheatcroft County Primary. Pupils didn't gather en masse to scream, 'Run, Tonky, Run' as I scorched round the track Forrest Gump-style. It was just a small but solid, private epiphany as I came to the end of my first 800-metre run, a mere two laps round the track but the longest I'd attempted thus far. A feeling of *Oh, this is something I can do* – new information as I contemplated the transition to secondary school.

Scalby Comprehensive was on the other side of town. I didn't know anyone there and, like many state schools of the '70s, it combined highly variable academic attainment with alarmingly consistent rates of violence at break. Bullying was rife. Gangs marauded the corridors, distributing dead arms and dead legs with psychopathic abandon. Underpants were savagely yanked to the ceiling with the cry of 'Shreddies!' On one occasion I saw a poor young lad having his hands forcibly held on a hot pipe in the cloakroom till he was physically sick with pain. Good times!

Fights happened on most days. To be hard was everything, and a solid hierarchy had been fought for and established on the gravelly playground. Acko was the hardest, the Peters brothers were up there, Blanchard, Pickering. Sometimes a new kid on the block would announce himself with a stunningly random act of violence, then the tectonic plates would shift, and he'd be called out to see if it was repeatable. If so, the table would adjust to the new member.

Looking back, the school was a bit of a hothouse for boxing excellence. Richard Dunn's son went to it. Richard Dunn had fought Muhammed Ali for the heavyweight championship of the world, big news for a Scarborough lad. The reward for his son was to fight a rotating sequence of challengers seemingly every lunchtime for months, defending a throne he neither deserved nor wanted. The whole school would gather round behind the RE portakabin to watch the action jumping up and down screaming: 'Scrap! Scrap! Scrap!' Dunn's son invariably won. Then there were the Ingle family, top scrappers. John, Michael and young Paul, who later went on to fight Naseem Hamed for the IBF featherweight championship of the world. I was there when Paul found his calling, narrowly avoiding a skirmish myself. What with regular visits from local schools to establish who was hardest at an interschool level (Macko from Raincliffe, Aitkens from Graham), it was exciting times on the North East coast.

My own fighting calibre was weak to terrible. At primary school I'd been a bit of a player, but the leap in standards and the size of the older kids caught me out. As a first year I got a black eye very quickly from a second year. It was the first time I'd been solidly bashed in the face, a shocking sensation. A year later, I gallantly stepped in to protect some girls from a lad three years my elder. Seeing the injustice of his taunts, I grabbed hold of his shirt, ran down some stairs with him and smashed his back against some railings. This hurt my opponent, and, looking back, I should have capitalised on the moment. But I didn't. I paused, wondering what the next move was, still holding his shirt as if adjusting his tie on the morning of a wedding. Turns out the next move was for the lad to punch me very hard in my hard head. My head hit the even harder wall, at which point I sat down and began, as they said up north at the time, to 'beef' (cry). Pretty soon, he was beefing as

9

well. Turns out he had broken his hand on my head. On balance I'm claiming it as a win.

Like all kids at secondary school, I realised that if I were to survive, or maybe even thrive, an angle was needed.

Turns out I was reasonably funny. To this day I am eternally grateful to my physics teacher, Mr Foot. I had lessons with him every Tuesday morning and was always late. This meant an excuse was needed (beyond I just don't like physics). Every week I'd come up with more outlandish reasons to explain my tardiness, or even just mundane ones; the important thing is they were funny, the class would be in stitches. Pretty soon I was being late just to tell the excuses. Being a thoroughly good sport, Mr Foot saw the fun I was having and would often give me the floor before the lesson started, ushering me to the front of the class to offer up the latest wild tale for the entertainment of the assembled. A win for everyone. I got to make people laugh, which is always pleasurable, and my classmates got to postpone physics, a subject that nobody seemed to like – including, I suspect, Mr Foot.

So comedy was emerging as part of my character, but I knew it wouldn't be enough. It's a subjective form, you can't make everyone laugh and sometimes harder kids would give you a clump in passing just for being clever. It was sport that truly defined me – football in the winter, tennis in the summer, and throughout the year, running. My first year at Scalby I quickly secured my status as the fastest at cross-country. To be fair, it was a crown that nobody else wanted, cross-country being universally despised. Every four weeks, one of the PE teachers, either the stately, more traditional, rugby-playing Mr Holden or the slightly more roguish football-playing Mr Fletcher, would walk us jovially to the start of the school cross-country course before outlining the course for their own entertainment. It started at the bottom of a brutally sharp hill and continued in a similarly confront-ational manner for approximately 4½ miles. The scene was undeniably Kes-like as the horrendously steep, 600-metre (2,000-foot) hill halfway round would be described gleefully as a 'slight incline' to shivering kids. No weather would stop us; in fact, often we'd run cross-country when the weather was too cold or wet for football, the reasoning being that the teachers could start proceedings before retiring to the shed for tea, or in Fletcher's case, a fag. Invariably I'd barrel to the front and stay there in my slip-on black gym pumps, black shorts and light blue school football top. I was that oft misunderstood outlier at school, the kid who liked cross-country.

It was all part of a life devoted to movement. I'd wake at 6, run to the newspaper shop, run my paper round, then cycle 4 miles across town to school. PE at school, football every break, cycle home, run another paper round. I just loved motion. It is these years, I imagine, that set your internal engine for life. Even now, occasionally as an adult I'll just run to a location fully dressed because I fancy it; it reminds me of the boundless energy and simplicity of youth. At that age I would run everywhere, but strangely, I never *went* for a run, on my own. For some reason it had never formalised into something I could just decide to do.

And then one day, it did.

It was the early summer of 1981, the middle of the summer holidays. I was 12, having completed my first year at secondary school. At a loose end, in an empty house and with no tasks at hand, I thought, *I could just go now, I could leave this, just go for a run. I like running.* It was a delicious prospect. *Why not just do it?*

So I did.

Scarcely able to breathe, such was my excitement, I hurriedly strapped on a pair of white Dunlops, put on a pair of bright red shorts and a deep blue string vest that I was wearing at the time, and took to the streets. No need to warm up at 12, just out.

We lived on the south side of town, and it was a gentle downhill mile or so down the wide Esplanade, bordered with freshly mowed grass lawns, ornately landscaped for the tourist crowd that packed the South Side. The weather was baking as I weaved through, my plimsolls slapping the smooth grey paths as I descended across the Spa Bridge, turned right at the Grand Hotel and then quickstepped down about 10 flights of steep steps onto the beach at the height of summer season.

I remember feeling increasingly calm as I found my rhythm. Amid the kids screaming, the crying of seagulls, the twirling cascades of arcade machines and the ruddy-faced fisherman selling mini pots of shrimp and touting for harbour trips out on the bay, it felt good, as if something was shifting inside me, dissolving. In the effortless turning of my legs beneath me, the pumping of my thin childlike arms, a startling peace was opening up within, a fantastical lift that sent me soaring through the sweet shops on the front, gliding past the Futurist theatre advertising Jimmy Tarbuck, Jaconelli's ice cream parlour, the donkeys and the ghost trains; propelled me away from that, up onto the Marine Drive, a gloriously flat, barren stretch of road linking the South beach to the North beach.

High-pitched screaming of fairground rides and caged trampolines quickly gave way to a spacious, intoxicating silence punctuated by the cries of distant seagulls. Sharp tangs of candy floss and popcorn were replaced by seaweed and the salty strength of the North Sea.

It was at this stage I saw how far I was going. If I went to the end of the drive and back it would be – how long? I had no idea. Long long. Unusually long. On I went. I'd found something, a sweet spot, a new vantage point from which to view life, and wanted to extend it. I plunged on recklessly in the heat, burning myself under the relentless sun, greedily sucking in air as the clear North Sea lightly sprayed my face. Reaching the end of the Drive, I paused for a second.

The sense of freedom was utterly intoxicating. I could go anywhere now; I didn't need anyone or anything, only the wit to depart and the fitness to carry it off. I could claim this, make it mine. I turned and launched myself back, loving it, every second; the tiredness in the limbs, the dry thirst in my mouth, the honest sweat caking my shoulders and back.

On my return I took a different route, my run degenerating to a lazy jog as I detoured round the spa in front of Max Jaffa's Open Air Concert Hall and the outdoor swimming pool. Then a swift turn right, zigzagging up the coastal paths, through the lustrous planted Italian Gardens to the clock tower by the pitch and putt. I was slowing a bit by now, excitement had faded. But I had found something, of that I was certain. Life had irrevocably changed. It was the b of the bang of my life as a runner, which continues to this day. Within two months I'd join Scarborough Harriers, and begin racing over country and on the track. At 12 years old, the last piece of my emerging identity had clicked into place. On some profound level, I had found both escape and salvation, I felt that very clearly – but as home came closer, a familiar dread was descending. I'd been out a long time without permission. Although unquestionably right for me, it was hard to defend.

As I turned the last corner homewards, I knew I'd shortly pay the price.

My hands trembled involuntarily as I opened the front gates; a creeping numb sensation ran up into my throat. Maybe it'd be fine, was the house empty?

No.

As I went round the back, I sensed movement indoors. Then, the insistent thudding of clogs firing off the kitchen floor (a sound that quickens my pulse to this day). A familiar form marched past the window.

I reached for the door but, before I got there, with a sharp click, it flew open.

London Marathon. Mile 1

Goal time – 00:06:48. Actual time – 00:06:56

Finally, fantastically, the field breaks free from the front, one body gently rupturing into component parts. The relief is ridiculous. All waiting is over, we're running now, just running. The paraphernalia falls away, swamped by this crushingly simple activity. Runners running, a sea of bobbing heads setting off from Greenwich, separating into 45,000 different stories.

It's funny, the first mile of a marathon. You're looking for your rhythm. There's nothing tiring in it, no exertion. It's searching for a groove, in the middle of a stream of runners doing exactly the same thing. You've spent months preparing this running machine and now it's getting a test run. It's like Christmas Day morning as a kid when everyone's in the park with their new bikes and jackets, showing off to an extent – and in the case of the marathon, trying not to waste too much energy dodging other runners, changing pace. I ease off to the left of the road and am quickly in tandem with Hoggy. The crowd cheers us on gently, nothing too serious at this point, more of a greeting. This section feels almost like a comedy intro. Everyone knows that the drama lies further down the road. They are cheering the fact that we've been daft enough to set off in the first place. It's good to see the start, an optimistic outpouring of humans clad in vest and shorts. Every now and again, we crest a speed bump in the road and let out a collective cheer – of fun, but also of warning to runners behind us. You don't want to be pulling a muscle on a bloody speed bump!

I see faces I know in the throng. Runners I've connected with on social media. It's a laugh to see them waving on the other side of the road as we set off on that long journey to The Mall. My legs are full of energy, strong and bouncy, bursting with four months of training and three days of carb-loading. My steps land featherlike in my brand-new shoes; there's an almost overwhelming temptation to sprint forward, but it's important not to. I've got to get the pacing right, it's like holding back a puppy.

The race hasn't really started yet, but Hoggy's starting to irritate me. And though it sounds clichéd, I know it's true: it's not him, it's me. On the face of it, running together should make sense. He's a club mate, after all, I like him, we've got loads in common. He seems comfortable enough; swapping club gossip as he dashes along next to me, innocently clutching a bag of hard-boiled sweets. I blame myself, it's the old enemy: overthinking. I've been stewing on this for months, every step of it, it's all been contemplated exhaustively, every phase, including this, the first mile or so. There's a need to stay totally relaxed, hydrated – cucumber cool. The truth is, I hadn't factored in Hoggy. Our strides don't quite align perfectly, his are longer than mine, it's slightly discordant. The chat as well; it's perfectly pleasant, but I'm having to concentrate ever so slightly on it, and that's mental energy I can't afford. I'd planned a solitary journey, a private quest. He's crashing my movie! It's also very hard to gauge pace if you're with someone else. If you're running fractionally too slow, but at someone else's cadence, it can tire you out. The motor needs to turn naturally, without thinking. It's crucial to conserve energy, just float through the first few miles, disengage. Basically, the arrangement's not working out: 20 miles of this and we'll be chucking each other in the Thames. How crazy, that after all the training I'd scupper myself by running with a mate. I never race with mates, it's a contradiction in terms. You've got to be captain of your own ship, for goodness' sake. What was I thinking?

All this is nibbling away at my brain as we approach the first mile. I haven't checked my watch yet, but I will, it's important to get an early reading, I glance down: 00:06:52/53 as we breeze past. Then, clocking off the first mile, 00:06:56.

Too slow.

That's it. I pronounce this experiment over. Not to be overdramatic, but I am not going to jeopardise this marathon on the altar of club camaraderie!

With a swift adieu to Hoggy, I'm off.

3

2 January. Flat white orgy

A wise man once said, *every day is a life*. If you think about it, he's right, sort of. Assuming the previous day hasn't taken too much of a toll, there is a feeling of renewal, we awake reborn. It's amazing what you can do in a day, especially with a bit of zest, and an ounce of good old-fashioned determination. Yesterday, begone with your slothful habits, procrastination and weird moods! Today is a new day. We begin again.

New Year's Day magnifies the reboot tenfold. Today will be different because it's a symbol of this year, which will be radically different. Ding ding – all change! I open the curtains and sing my barbaric yawp out into this wondrous universe, clad in my spanking new pyjama–slipper combo. I am unlimited, all powerful. With my new mindset and gratitude journal at hand, I intend to spend every living second in conscious union with all living beings, a humble servant of my fellow – wait, is that a notification on my iPhone? Quick, turn it off. I will not be enslaved by its vacuous allure. In fact, I'll use it for good. Let's try a TED Talk, an inspiring TED Talk to set me off. Google Ted. Bundy? No. Sheringham, YouTube highlights – golden goals. There goes half an hour. Work in a minute, let's just check Facebook. What a twat! I'm hungover anyway, nobody starts New Year on 1 January, get real. Where's that Christmas pudding in the fridge?

I love beginning again, but New Year can be a tad confrontational.

The real issue is, I'm coming off Christmas, which means I'm weaning myself off booze. Now, some runners sail through the Christmas season nibbling almonds and sipping sparkling mineral water, emerging fresh-faced and bushy-tailed into the New Year with a spring in their step. I tend to celebrate the Lord in a different fashion. Maybe chastened by Richard's onslaught, I felt my resolve fade as the warmth of Yuletide descended on the land. I drove to see a good friend who runs a wine shop in Walthamstow on 12 December, spent far too much money on a case of wine, went home and remarkably managed to race through it by the 18th before making the return journey to my astonished friend, who trousered yet more cash.

We're going to have to talk about this because it would be remiss not to mention my affectionate relationship with the bottle. Red wine's my tipple of choice. You will often find me of a Sunday afternoon perusing the shelves of my local Oddbins as if striding round the Louvre. As a working-class Northerner prone to moments of largesse, I have completely fallen for the faux sophistication of the wine connoisseur. It's all booze, of course; it's just that wine feels different. The bottles are given depth by the beguiling descriptions of the concoction within; their tattered mysterious labels offer the veneer of sophistication. Cocooned by this artistry, I am easily seduced. The staff at Oddbins greet me as a friend; in fact, they often run out to meet me. (My appearance at the shop invariably coincides with a bonus.) The blackboard signs outside seem to be addressed to me personally, the bottles call out: *Paul, take me home, I am available for decanting.* In the gloriously oaky library of booze, I find myself drifting from bottle to bottle, playing them off against each other like lovers, comparing regions and vineyards, my ears ringing with the seductive endorsements of informative staff members. *Taste this. Velvety undertones. Complex aftertaste, that one.* It's all a delightful ruse, of course; a process that invariably ends with me swaying in the corner of the kitchen four hours later, shadow-boxing by the fridge as I experiment with cheese and ham.

Because of my work schedule, I don't drink on a Friday or Saturday night, so Sunday becomes my default Big Night In. A weekly staycation. Relieved that the responsibilities in the field of entertainment are over for another week, I collapse on the sofa with a couple of bottles, for a boxset-athon. Let's be fair, this has given me great pleasure through the years; it's just, after a mere 12 years or so, it's started to pale. Part of the problem is that my dear wife invariably falls asleep mid-bottle, and I am forced to drink the remaining wine on offer. All manner of restraint quickly disappears and, before you know it, I am a housebound drunk buffoon. It is at this stage of the evening that I fall prey to a giddy but pointless triumphalism. I actually feel like I've achieved something. Carried on a tide of alcoholic bonhomie, another side of me springs forth; released from my naturally cautious nature, I reach out to the world. I tweet about football, confess admiration for public figures directly on social media and, to compound the madness, I google. I make plans, enter races, apply to online courses. This can complicate the inevitable hangover the following morning.

One morning I awoke dry-mouthed and heavy-headed to a phone call from a lovely Jewish gentleman in New York congratulating me on my decision to study Hebrew online. What could I say – 'Sorry, I was two bottles in'? Seconds later, an entry to the Mont Blanc Ultra pinged through on my email, followed quickly by a note from Amazon – Plato's *Republic* 'has been dispatched'. Who is this lunatic? This Jewish, ultrarunning classicist? Whoever he is, he certainly isn't me. I'm from Scarborough, Classics bores me and I'm not exactly sure where Mont Blanc is.

I don't drink often, but when I drink, I drink. *Capisce?*

Of course, to make the situation worse, with age, the hangovers hit harder, less a physical feeling, more of an existential crisis, a deeply melancholic, metaphysical, day-long dance with the idea of death. The most humdrum of tasks provoking a profound, tragicomic mental fragility. *I've got to go to the tip. To throw things out. Pack the car and drive there on my own. What gives me the right to choose which items get saved and which don't make the cut? What's this lampshade ever done? OK, it's dysfunctional – I'm dysfunctional. Shall I just throw myself out? Prostrate myself like a fallen angel in the non-recyclable items to be crushed into landfill, just like I've (gulp) been crushed by life?*

Running has been a godsend in this regard, a corrective to my excesses. The perfect hangover cure is an easy run through the woods, communion with nature, the sanctity of sweat; but I wanted this year to be different.

This year, **no booze till the marathon**. Or failing that, at the very least I was joining the Dry January movement. Easily said, but if achieved, it would be by far the longest I've gone without booze since records began.

Honesty was required. Awareness. I had to realise that the Oddbins staff weren't my friends. They were evil enablers. The building itself wasn't a benevolent treasure chest of sophisticated pleasure, it was a portal to a mindless bedlam. It had to be resisted. From this day forth, I had to summon the will to walk past Oddbins.

Athletically, I knew it would make a difference. Although I could run off a hangover, it was never a good run. The muscles are weak, you are prone to strains, injury. How can there be the bounce in the legs when you're literally poisoned? I had to do it. Give myself half a chance.

I was also slightly tubbier than usual, by about a stone. It's not just the booze. At Christmas, I eat all the stuff that you're meant to eat at Christmas. Turkey and all the trimmings, especially the trimmings – aren't they the best bits? That gloopy syrupy slick of bounteous joy on your plate at the end of a Christmas dinner, that cranberry-infused elixir of stuffing-drenched bliss. That has to be good for you, right? The next morning you might find me scoffing a mince pie for breakfast or partaking in my discovery of last season, salted caramel Florentines – which, I discovered, go very well with cheese, as do most fruit cakes and, shamefully, chips and chicken. It's basically a scorched earth policy of any visible food eaten in any combination and it had resulted in a fatty deposit encircling my waist.

I looked at it on the evening of 1 January with a steely resolve; it had to go.

This year a plan was solidifying in my mind. I was going to run the marathon faster than ever, wrestle with the beast, win even, if that was possible. Tonight, sober and full of salad, I would sleep the sleep of the righteous. Tomorrow, 2 January, the New Year would begin, with a trip to good old Coffee Circus.

Now, Crouch End, the setting for much of this drama, occupies the strange cultural hinterland between Hampstead and Archway in North London. It's a funny little semi-affluent pocket of the world. No Tube, but serviced by the W7 sneaking up from Finsbury. The population is a mixed bunch: the moneyed and the cashless, the drugged-up and the kale-munching, Manuka-honey-dripping farmers' market brigade. A dizzying array of shop fronts testify to the wildly varying disposable incomes and temperaments of residents. You'll find gastro pubs competing with good old-fashioned boozers, artisan bakers going toe to toe with Greggs. There are bookies, four dry cleaners, three banks, a Co-op, a Waitrose, Marks & Spencer and Tesco Express within 400 metres, all battling for the passing pound alongside assorted chuggers, beggars and street characters. It's a lovely village, I feel lucky to live there, and the celebs reflect the nature of the place. Lots of comedians you may or may not have heard of; that odd diamond Sean Hughes lived here (RIP); Alan Carr stopped off for a few years; there was Simon Pegg (pre-Hollywood), as well as several Dr Whos (Capaldi and Tennant), all nipping in and out of the cafés that exert a caffeinated stranglehold over the place. That's the real retail story of the area: coffee wars. Cafés constantly appearing. In fact, within 200 square metres at the bottom of the hill, just down from Oddbins (why must I use this as my frame of reference?), there are five outlets. Three big corporations, one Italian deli restaurant place, and the fairly new arrival – and my personal favourite – Coffee Circus.

First things first. The title is deceiving; very few circus skills are on offer in Coffee Circus. Nobody's tumbling and I have yet to see a lion. What it does do is concentrate solely on the coffee. It's independent, there's very little food on offer, it's an inconveniently narrow but usually very busy supplier of rocket fuel magic to kickstart the bodies and minds of the menagerie of humankind that goes in there: stressed mums enjoying the post-school drop-off pre-hot yoga window, ultra-thin creative types working on projects, bored trust fund slobs chatting to the staff, and a rolling ragbag of degenerates, decorators, doctors, daily diehards, anyone who loves coffee.

To me, it's the beating heart of the area and 2 January found me sitting in my usual seat facing the door, sipping a flat white, reading my *Times* and getting ready to attack. I was on it. ON IT. The to-do list was a mile long; just to look at it was inspirational. I couldn't wait to race through it, yup, over the top into the New Year, immediately after completing the *Times* quick crossword, a process that normally takes about two hours.

'All right, mate.'

It was Roisin Conaty bursting through the door – comedian, actor, writer and all-round media player. She's a bubbly bright bundle of Irish Cockney fun who I tend to bump into three times a year max, either here or, bizarrely, in front of the cold meats in Marks & Spencer. For it to happen at the beginning of this brave new dawn felt like a message. She quickly sat down and a New Year's resolution roast battle began.

I opened with a Dry January.

Roisin sensationally twisted with a Dry *Year*.

What? A Dry Year!?

I was gobsmacked, but she seemed resolute. It felt so good, she said, the previous year when she'd stopped for a few months, that drinking just made no sense. She had so many projects to do. Why do it? Why self-sabotage? Her eyes shone with fervour; she'd spent some time in the States and radiated LA positivity. Everything seemed so simple, why not a year? Emboldened by her audacity, we ordered another flat white each and ski-jumped off into the rarefied atmosphere of New Year affirmations and self-help jargon.

Diet?

We were both going to lose weight – that was obvious. No booze is a good start, but bread was on the ropes for both of us. Vegetables were ascending, closely followed by oily fish, nuts, purple-sprouting broccoli. Cheese was in danger of never being seen again. And biscuits! Sweets! As for chocolate, we laughed uproariously at the notion. NO! It made no sense. Why put something into your body that it didn't need and couldn't use? This year would be different, we would be *our own best friends*. Imagine how you'd feel if you only made right choices. We *could create ourselves*, we *could design the life we wanted*. So we did, in Coffee Circus.

Projects?

We listed them all. Scripts! Shows! Material! All it needed was a daily commitment to the creative process. We knew what held us back – procrastination, social media nonsense. (I almost chipped in *masturbation during the day*, but I didn't want to say that out loud in case it set off a tsunami of self-abuse in the very suggestible atmosphere that was developing.) Again, just junk for the brain. No thanks. Not this year. *Attention was to the mind what activity was to the body.* We would guard the contents of our mind, use our time wisely. No sharing of a meaningless status on Facebook. We would forge our status in the white heat of the real world, we would look at it steely eyed, make rational decisions. Roisin was on fire with it all. The buzz was ON.

A third flat white hardly touched the sides. It was, I quickly realised, an overreach. My heart immediately began to bump so hard I felt it might splurge out my chest like John Hurt in *Alien*.

'What's your main aim this year?' Roisin squeaked, rocking in her chair, possibly on the verge of a panic attack.

'A fast marathon,' I blurted out. 'It feels unfinished.' This was a serious, true point, which might have carried more dignity if I hadn't been reflexively tapping out repetitive beats on the table at the time with the coffee spoon.

'Good. What would that look like? You need to be specific. It needs to be measurable. S.M.A.R.T. – specific, measurable, achievable, realistic and you need a time frame.' Roisin *had* been to the States, she was good.

'I don't know.'

'You do. You do know. We always know. What would it be? How long would it take?' She was pointing now, pressing the point, though it might have been an exaggerated twitch.

'I don't. Honestly, no idea. It's about the process, it's about me and the distance.'

'That's not good enough. You know. You're scared. I can see it.' Her eyes lasered into me like a flat white truth ray.

I felt suddenly exhausted and my eyes drifted off sharply leftwards. Roisin's gaze tracked mine, locking in. We were now both utterly transfixed by the cake stand. Decisions, in every moment. Decisions define moments, which add up to define days, years, lives. It's not the cake, it's what the cake represents. We're surrounded by symbols. Can we resist?

If I was going to do this, run this time that I wanted but could barely verbalise, I was going to have to train harder than ever, I was going to have to do that most difficult thing: actually change.

Roisin grabbed the bull by the horns. She stood up, put her bag on her shoulder and held the bill above her head as if lifting a trophy. 'I've got this!'

4

4 January. In da club

Structures needed to be put in place for the year's ascent; harnesses and pegs strewn across the mountainous marathon schedule. One of these without a doubt would be club training on a Tuesday, for to scale any peak, it's always best to be attached to other people. (Here ends the marathon as mountain metaphor.)

For the pure runners out there, I give one piece of advice. To get fitter, faster and enjoy your running more, I say simply: join a club. Tap into the expertise of its members, run a variety of distances and experience the camaraderie and fun that an excruciatingly taxing training session can bring. It's amazing what the security of numbers can do for the mind. To run alone is a wonderful pleasure; medicinal, relaxing and refreshing on a soul level. But for actual training, company is all; you can lodge yourself in the centre of the pack and hold on as long as possible, being carried to unfeasible speeds.

The first session of the year was a tentative reunion with collective pain. A quick glance round the group indicated that I was definite winner of the Runner Who'd Let Themselves Go Most Over Christmas Award. Other club members talked a good game about how they'd let things slide but they still looked whippet slim. Most of them are a singular breed: thin-bodied practical types, gentle in conversation but fiercely competitive and fed by a wide cross-section of different jobs and social classes. You'll find doctors chasing down builders, lawyers battling with teachers, and, it has to be said, more than a smattering of civil servants. It was only three days in to Dry January; I had resisted Oddbins thus far, my mind was clearer, but the belly, my new mate, needed no formal introduction. We grouped, shivering, under the floodlights as club coach Jacob greeted us and outlined the night's session. To get technical for a minute: 2×1600 metre repetitions with short recoveries; a four-minute rest; then 8×400 metre reps, again with short recoveries.

Over the years the club has divided into three groups reflecting ability. A, B and, you've guessed it, C.

Group A occupy a different physical universe to the normal human: they are ridiculously fast, smooth-running, clear-eyed lunatics with a freakishly high pain threshold and not an ounce of fat between them. Less normal humans and more of an ideal to aspire to, they're examples of a higher state of being, living a monk-like ascetic existence, sustained by a diet of nuts, berries and pure oxygen.

Group B is fairly fast; some of its members are on the turn, either on the way to Group A or falling away from it. The transition from Group B to group A is extremely hazardous and rarely attempted, often ending in physical and psychological collapse.

Group C consists of improving runners, new club members adjusting to a new intensity and fairly normal members of society. The key to enjoying your running is finding your level. Group B is serious but not life-threatening. That first evening back, I set my stall out at its rear, hanging on for dear life towards the end of long reps as recyclable oxygen drained from my system, lactic acid invaded my limbs and I fought a desperate desire to be sick.

My spirit was willing, but the flesh was weak. The Christmas belly was a dead weight and times progressively deteriorated as the evening continued. There was absolutely nothing I could do about it. It's a nightmarish moment when runners glide away in front of you, their backs inexorably fading round the bend, slowly being swallowed by a distant darkness. You kid yourself at first, you say, *I'll catch them up in a minute, I'm just coasting, lulling them into a false sense of security.* It's a delusion, of course, this idea that you have any control over the matter. If you were going to catch them up, why let them run off in the first place? Why not just stay with them like you normally do? Oh, we love a fiction. The truth is, you're unfit, your legs are a dead weight. This is the Xmas Florentine forfeit. I am once again reminded of actions and consequences. It is hard at this moment but essential not to fall prey to a profound self-pity; it's a tough moment, that's all. As Kipling said, 'If you can fill the unforgiving minute / With sixty seconds' worth of distance run,' etc. Trouble is, the length of recoveries compounds the problem. Intervals are timed on the fastest runner, which means that as you fall behind, recovery times get shorter and shorter, you're more tired when you set off for the next one, so you tumble further behind, which shortens the recoveries even more. It's like bad debt. You're caught in a Wonga spiral of accumulating lactic acid. No shame in being last in the group, certainly no judgement from others. We've all been there; it's just that on that particular night it's you.

When the torture was over, I jogged round with club mates as bile collected ominously in the back of my throat. We discussed aims for the year. A small gang had entered the London marathon: Hoggy, Dom, Gavin and Sarah. The idea of a sub-3 marathon was mooted. A sub-3 marathon is the golden grail for many club athletes, an achievable but desperately elusive barrier, something akin to an everyman's 4-minute mile. My personal best was 03:03:52 run at York the previous year. At the time it had felt like the run of my life, impossible to go faster. Dom had been wrestling with a sub-3 for years; he's a graceful, high-stepping, rake-thin athlete, way faster than me over road, track and country – it's all in the glide with him. His PB stood at a fantastically awful 03:00:24 – absurdly close. In Dom's case the battle seemed to have become more psychological than physical. His face painted a picture of benign confusion as we contemplated our prospects while stretching trackside.

'It's like I've done it already, really,' Dom offered. 'Twenty-four seconds. It's less than a second a mile, so you could say I've already run a sub-3 marathon.'

The group paused a while, as this obvious unreality sailed up to the moon, along with the remnants of Dom's sanity. We wanted to be supportive, but – was somebody going to tell him? The incontrovertible sign of a sub-3 marathon is the fact that it takes less than three hours. Those 24 seconds may be only seconds, but those seconds do actually count.

'I mean, it's basically nothing. On another watch, you've done it,' Dom continued.

This was getting worse. What was this other watch? What unit of time did it measure? Could we dial it back to the '90s and become magically younger, faster?

It's at times like this you need a South African. Luckily, we had one. Gavin. 'The problem is, you don't believe you can do it. You have to believe it deep down, and the very first step to that, of course, is accepting the fact that you haven't done so already. You've got to be honest with yourself.'

Gavin gazed at us across a boundless chasm: he'd run *numerous* sub-3 marathons, with a PB of 02:49:23, as such he brought news from a Promised Land. He was the oldest, fastest and hardest among us – a 56-year-old, muscular, academic, pit bull pocket rocket, who seemed to conduct himself with an absolute contempt for normal bodily limitations. Famous at the club for ignoring injuries, he once fell on a training weekend, bashed his head on some rocks, ignored expert advice strongly advising him to seek medical attention, fashioned a makeshift bandage from plasters and running socks, and strapped up for another day on the fells. He has a Trump-like ability to live in his own reality – but don't tell him I said that, he hates Trump with a passion. The point is, when he talks running, you listen.

'There's no point being wishy-washy about it, you've got to say you can do it – get that message into your subconscious. I **am** going to do it. I **am** going to run sub-3 hours for the marathon. It's a mental journey first.'

This was bold, confrontational language for the first Tuesday club track of the year. Hoggy broke out into a smile and set off on another couple of laps to warm down. Sarah nodded in agreement; she was another member of the sub-3 brigade.

'I agree,' she said. 'It's a state of mind'.

'I think I can do it,' Dom uttered, perched rather precariously on his bike, ready to cycle home. 'I do. I really think I can.'

'Not good enough, I'm afraid,' Gavin piped up. 'That's defeatist. You have to know it. Say it out loud, and believe it. You mark your own territory. No point thinking it.'

At that point, I excused myself and sauntered off to the trackside changing rooms. I thought I was about to be sick. Within 20 seconds I believed I was going to be. Gavin was right. You have to believe it. I didn't say it out loud because I didn't want to tell anyone, but deep down I knew. Soon it was no longer deep down; bending over the toilet bowl, sweating heavily, nausea sprang forth.

I was marking my own territory.

5

Two days later. Bryony Gordon drags us south of the river

Club night had sent me spinning philosophically on the nature and connection between the mental and physical in running. Dom and Gavin had viewpoints I could easily understand, I recognised myself in both. In the past, I had wholeheartedly embraced Dom's stance, but there was also an inner Gavin, buried deep inside me. Whichever approach I took, it had to ring true. That, I realised, was the main thing; I'd had wild behaviour swings before.

Who could forget the long, sober and hideously dull summer of 2004, followed by the drunkest October in living memory? The breadless and joyless spring of 2008? More recently, the ill-thought-out flirtation with the Stone Age paleo diet? That eight-day carbless hell, which ended suddenly as I burst into tears midway through serving up the kids' potato smiley faces?

Any change had to make sense. It couldn't be a quick fix. No crazy goals. The sub-3 thing was bothering me slightly. It was a tempting idea, but I knew how tough it would be, I wasn't ready to go all in. In my life I'd always worked hard for balance. *Everything in moderation but moderation* had become a proverb I quoted frequently. It's a deceptively difficult, quite extreme position. I sought to dance with light steps twixt debauchery and denial. For now, I was feeling better; it was a time for baby steps.

The weekly podcast (Running Commentary – recorded – for runners, by runners *while running*) broke up the week's training in a very natural fashion. It was a day when I knew I'd be running and chatting with someone else, pleasure guaranteed. To me this is about as good as life gets, a long slow run/chat with mates, preferably in the woods. The kernel of the show had been Rob and I enjoying chatting while running and noticing that as the run got longer, the endorphins would fire and our chat would soar off into the outer reaches of idiocy and philosophical thought. It was actually mid-run when the idea came to us. We'd hit that phase of a good run when you feel you can run endlessly: all was bright and good, our feet and thoughts wonderfully cushioned by soft woodlands, our ideas lifted by the explosion of autumnal colour that surrounded us.

If we can get a bit Zen for a moment, I always feel that a good run opens you out into a parallel time system: after 40 minutes or so, time assumes a fluid nature; you've discovered and burst through a portal into a deeper connection to life. Moments can be sunk into, they can splinter and flow in directions hitherto unimaginable. It's a moment-to-moment awareness, a deep union with all living things. If I were Eckhart Tolle, I'd call it the eternal moment, but I'm not so I'll call it as near to heaven on Earth as is possible. Bliss certainly. A transitory glimpse of paradise. At times like this, conversation isn't an exchange of ideas, it's a free-form enterprise, a sharing of light observations, revelations, completely unforced. The solitary *you* has become a shared *we*. It was at the very peak of such a run that we flawed humans – comedians, indeed – had an extremely unspiritual thought: we could do this as a podcast! Why not formalise this? Take this innocent natural activity and turn it into a product?

So we did, and the chat initially got a bit tense and stilted, not helped by the fact that the recorders didn't work. Then we chilled out, found the right tech, the chat returned, and now it flows across a variety of media platforms. Every week we do one, every week it goes out. Running Commentary. The community is ever growing and supportive, it's immensely pleasurable to do and we just about break even, so it's a win-run situation.

Another great thing about it is you get to meet funny, interesting people. That February morning had been marked in red for a while, for that was the day that Deering and I chipped down to Clapham to do a recording with Bryony Gordon.

I'd been a fan of Bryony's books and columns for a long time. Her writing is brilliant: warm, honest and funny. She ushered us into her tastefully decked-out Clapham terraced house, the type beloved by young media couples, and we coffeed quickly before setting off into a fresh morning.

Cheerfully announcing that she was 'built for comfort not for speed', Bryony immediately confessed to smoking a packet of menthol cigarettes the day before. We collectively came to the conclusion that this was akin to salad for the lungs, and she led the way round her normal Clapham Common loop in a plethora of apologies over *not being very fast*, while exhorting us to *feel free to run ahead*. This would stretch the parameters of our flimsy tech to breaking point, so we assured her the idea was to stick together. After 10 minutes or so we settled into a relaxed run/walk pattern punctuated by the occasional hop and a skip over a condom or syringe that littered the common; we were, after all, in South London. It's the Wild West down there, anything's possible.

For every runner, the path to running is different; there's often a before and after, a journey from sloth to champion. Bryony's had quite the trip. The previous year, while writing her very well received *Mad Girl*, a tale of her emergence from and life with the mental illness OCD, she'd had a bit of a relapse. 'Who'd have thought that writing about being mentally ill might make you mentally ill again?' Old thought patterns had renewed their terrifying assault; feelings of panic and anxiety had returned. Running had helped: on a basic level, in terms of brain chemistry, the increase of endorphins had added to her happiness. The language Bryony used was starkly humorous, and a tad self-deprecating; a 20-minute run was described as basically 'trying to stay alive', but I could tell she enjoyed it. She cut an inspiring figure on our syringe steeplechase, gleefully regaling us with tales of drunken excess, which I tried hard to understand. What is this booze of which you speak? What effects does it have on the mind? For Bryony, alcohol was down to once a week; control had been asserted in every area. It was when she swelled with pride sharing the tale of her running 10k on Christmas Day that I saw she was in the middle of real change: running can do this. It can rescue you. A year ago, she had been bedbound, depressed, imprisoned by repetitive, self-sabotaging behaviours. Now she was laughing and running. She shared with us her greatest breakthrough, when she saw that nobody else cared about her pace. It was all utterly relative. This was great podcast material, being a central tenet of our show, a maxim even: *anyone who runs is a runner, at any speed.* It's yours. Claim it. Seek to improve if you want, but only for yourself. See it as a gift to yourself, an appointment of pleasure rather than a masochistic date with an inner demonic taskmaster, especially in the early days.

Knowing that it had worked, feeling the results herself, Bryony had created Mental Health Mates, an idea for people with mental illness to meet up in parks and run or walk together. It was a pure idea born of the most generous of notions: people in trouble can find a place to be together and do something that makes them feel better. Unsurprisingly, it did very well; chapters sprang up round the UK, then the world. What with the sponsors of that year's London Marathon being Heads Together, a charity concerned with mental health, Bryony had hit a chord. There'd been invites to the Palace, tea with the royals, heady days. When we got back to the house, Bryony got the phone call from her agent saying she was at the top of the *Sunday Times* non-fiction bestseller lists that week. The zeitgeist was happening literally there, in the kitchen. She had lassoed the moon and we were there to see it, but we had to go: I still hadn't had a drink all month and champagne was imminent.

As we jogged back to the Tube, it seemed a done deal. The results were in. And dammit, it seemed that Richard was right. Pain did seem a consistent driver in people's motivations to run. Bryony had literally formed a worldwide organisation based on this very concept – and yet, most runners I knew were essentially happy folk. It's a chicken and egg scenario. Are runners happy because they run or depressed because they have to?

It was something I noticed at the club. The more that runners ran, the more they committed themselves to it, the happier and more relaxed they seemed. Bryony had touched on it mid-run. With running 'you get more physical pain, but it's offset by less mental pain when you're not running'.

There's a trade-off. Her comment made me focus in a bit on this relationship to pain. I began to see connections in my own reasons for running, and those of my club mates. Pain seemed to be something we were running from but also towards – and the faster we ran, the more pain we got, the faster we wanted to run.

Mile 3. Woolwich Arsenal. Shark in the water

Goal time – 00:20:55. Actual time – 00:21:02

Footsteps light? Check.

Arms relaxed? Check.

Stride length/tempo? All good.

I'm hydrated and in a state of running relaxation, there but not there, floating through a very wide dual carriageway in South London. It's a bit of a tease, those first few miles at London. There are a few long downhill stretches, along with the temptation to hit them hard. You must resist this! Just flow. You can pick up a few seconds without effort by letting yourself be gently seduced by gravity, but if at any point you feel that you're consciously speeding up, running fast, I'm afraid you're in the middle of a terrible mistake and you must return to the start. In the near distance I can see Vassos' rangy stride, he's locked in to his headphones; Hoggy can see me from a similar distance behind. It's a chain of sorts. By now, rhythm has been established; the engine created through months of training has turned over and is bedding in. The trick is to mentally switch off. Mental energy is finite, to be distributed with care. Some runners are getting a tad angry at water stations. It is a bit busy, there can be a scramble, but there doesn't have to be. London has water stations every mile, just chill through it. Of course, if you try too hard to float through everything, you get into the *I'm trying so hard to relax that I'm really stressed* trap and that's no good either. I remind myself – nothing's really happened yet. My legs feel great, no problems of any kind, I've got my gels in my pocket and miles to run. It will get heavy later, but for now, I try to react with the spectators. High-five a row of kids, enjoy the sound systems. Crowds are two or three deep by the side of the road; it's actually a good spot to watch, as it's the zone where all runners merge. Brits love a merge! The Green, Red and Blue, three streams of runners from three different starts, quickly blend and sift into one. The field fills up, meaning a temporary adjustment. Space crunches up for a while, there's strength in numbers. The mob has reached peak capacity. The mass marathon march swells and rolls on to the Palace.

Across the road from me I see fellow Heathsider Mario. Due to the idiosyncrasies of the starting system, he's started down the field from me and is making up for lost time. Mario breathes the rarified atmosphere of Group A on club nights; he's operating at a different level to me, chasing 2:45. I watch him from a distance, fascinated. Fast runners have a different form to me. However fit I get, I'll always be a scuttler. My style is a low arm carriage, low knee lift, round-shouldered affair. Under any kind of pressure, it quickly degenerates into a floppy, wasteful, sprawling parody. If you look at slow-motion replays of great athletes, their upper body is relaxed, their neck loose, faces soft and pliant. Under pressure, my neck seems to divide into grotesque tendrils and I never quite know what to do with my head. If I don't keep an eye on it it's lolling all over the place, the tongue's out, my face all scrunched up. When witnessing it, you can be under no illusion: this guy is trying his absolute hardest, he's knackered. Of course, it's really a sign of inefficiency; I'm trying no harder than anyone else. In fact, studies show that elite athletes at the head of the field are under more physical stress than those further down. They just mask it better.

Mario's stride has an effortless bounce that would exhaust me in minutes, the slight forward lean of his upper body is at a perfect angle as he eats up the ground, but it's his face that gets my attention. It's utterly focused, completely devoid of expression. In the moment but ferociously determined. He's in a different state, shall we call it Shark Zen? With one look he spies the most efficient way through the chaotic convergence that confronts him. I wave, but he doesn't see me; instead, he accelerates smoothly, slicing the pack open, his blue vest quickly disappearing in the rolling quilt of vests ahead. It's all a shockingly sharp contrast to me, lolloping along chilling to reggae and high-fiving toddlers. I need to step up, get my head in gear, key into this marathon business, it's not a kids' TV show. I drop my arms, take a deep breath, shake loose. Coming up to 5km. Another time check: 00:21:02.

That's better. Back on track now. This race is on. I'm nowhere near tired still, but form has been established, I've found my groove. No more high fives with the crowd. *Today's the day to get it all out. Nothing left at the end.* I surrender to the motion, quick, light, small steps, relaxed shoulders. I'm locked in.

It is the end of the beginning.

6

Mid February. McIntyre Mayr madness

It's hard to maintain determination for long. When running and in life generally.

New Year's Resolution Fever faded fast. It usually does. January is easy; you've got momentum behind you and the change is intoxicating. The body's enjoying the incredible novelty of a life without sugar, giving up booze is a relief. There's loads of stuff to be dealt with in early January, and clarity is needed. Who wants to be negotiating a new deal on car insurance when hungover? It's a relief to leave the alcoholic swamp behind – and you're getting things done. Let's join Costco! Go to the tip! Get the dogs a haircut! But February is the cruellest month, tasks are crossed off the to-do list, and sooner or later you're left with normality and its temptations. Cup of tea – and *biscuits*? Feeling peckish – nuts or *lovely buttery toast*? I'd reached the end of Dry January totally sober, dry as a cigar and crisp sandwich. Since then, cracks had appeared. I'd succumbed midweek the first week of February and shared a bottle with my wife, the enabler. I'd fought back vigorously and retained my distance, but resolution was fading: a glass here, a cheeky carafe there. The stride past Oddbins had degenerated into a forlorn shuffle, staff members glancing at me enticingly through the window (or were they just continuing about their business?). The blackboard signage outside seemed to be beckoning me in personally.

'Hey, Paulie, you've proved your point. How long must this charade continue? Come home!! Just a cheeky bottle.'

I knew I had to resist, be strong, but I was wavering. Look, there I am, gazing out into the garden. It's Sunday afternoon, 3.45 p.m. We're contemplating a roast. I'm on a knife-edge, the food-booze trigger is imminent and I'm about to throw in the towel. My wife's going to look at me with her gorgeous little face and ask me with a cheeky wink whether I fancy a 'little bottle'. I'm going to pretend to consider it for a moment before an 'OK' escapes from my lips, a low whisper of assent followed by that old lie 'Just one', but I know we are co-players in a fiction. We know what we're starting. We're doomed, I tell you; doomed!

We don't do 'a little bottle'. We'd buy a bottle, drink it unnaturally fast, then nip down and buy another, only to return an hour later well and truly on the guzzle, utterly seduced by booze's wicked spell. We'd bound back up the hill homewards, cackling like witches, triumphant and buoyant, setting sail into a night of glorious possibility. We'd saunter into the warm intoxicating joy of the living room, open the third bottle and start surfing Netflix to plan the evening's entertainment. Then quickly, while scrolling, energy would fade and my wife would pull her usual trick, the nodding head/glazed eye combo signalling the unmistakable slump. Before you know it, she'd be fast asleep on the sofa, barely into the last bottle. This would leave me alone and drunk, with nearly an entire bottle to deal with. Corkable certainly, but ridiculously drinkable, and with *Match of The Day 2* on the telly that's a no-brainer. Before you know it, *Match of the Day 2*'s finished and I'm crying uncontrollably in front of an old *24 Hours in A&E* that I've already watched. I've been mugged by and fallen victim to a Two Bottle Sunday. Which leads to a Still Drunk Monday Morning before limping into Abyss Tuesday and washing up on the shores of Where Have You Been All Week? Wednesday.

These decisions happen in a moment; in a split second they add up and define us. They condemn us to a life of sloth, non-achievement – and, impossible to deny, undeniable fun. What a laugh to surrender to booze, to sink into its velvety embrace! There's a devilish unconquerable logic to it. She's turning to me now with the beginnings of a grin, I can feel myself weakening and then, from nowhere, the Gods of Fortune surprise me: a phone call.

'Hello, mate!'

It was the familiar high-pitched falsetto of my good friend and showbiz legend, Michael McIntyre. Now listen, I know this feels like a huge name drop. It's not, I promise. I have very few showbiz mates, but he's undoubtedly one of them. We had the same agent years ago, got on as comics can – and, well, you'll make of it what you will.

It is a friendship that has survived seismic changes in our social and financial standing. At first, I was the senior partner. If not riding high, I was at least actually on television from time to time and was guiding the young, preternaturally talented Mac into the industry and a career of unimaginable fame and fortune. Think Newman and Cruise in *The Color Of Money*, Duvall and Penn in *Colors*. He was absolutely penniless in those days. It was a running joke how many meals I'd buy him. I remember on one occasion getting a reverse-charge phone call from Leicester Forest East Services. It was Michael; he'd filled up the car, but his card had been declined! Ten years later we're now in a scenario where he's Mr Saturday Night on prime-time BBC1 and could buy the entire station. His life is peppered with escapades only available to the rich and famous. Luckily for me, he often drags me along as a form of Northern mascot.

'What are you doing next week, mate?'

When Michael asks what I'm doing the following week, it is often the prelude to an experience well outside my income range. The next thing I know, I'm halfway round the world scoffing black cod, in the Royal Box at Wimbledon or at a Champions League final. 'What have you got in mind?'

'I'm thinking of going on a detox.'

'Whereabouts?' This sounded promising, it would boost my training.

'The Mayr clinic in Austria? Have you heard of it?'

I had heard of the Mayr clinic. There had been a spate of articles about it in the New Year, attesting to the simplicity and effectiveness of its treatments, the beauty of the surroundings, the eye-watering cost.

'Of course you have.' (In his mind I represent all things healthy – a psychological process known as projection.) 'Anyway, they have a revolutionary method of guaranteeing weight loss.'

'What's that?'

'It's very simple, they don't give you any food.'

'Nothing at all?'

'Not a sausage. Well, especially not a sausage.'

'Couldn't we just do that here?'

'The short answer to that is no. You've seen my relationship with fridges.'

I had indeed been privy to Michael on one of his late-night fridge forays. It was not an edifying spectacle.

'You do eat something, mostly stale bread.'

'It sounds good,' I replied. 'How would that work?'

'What do you mean? It's very simple. We go to Austria, they don't give us any food, we lose weight, we come home.'

'Yes, but—'

Finally he twigged. 'Oh, I'd pay! I wouldn't ask you to pay. You're doing me a favour. I can't do it alone, it's going to be torture.'

Saved literally by the bell. I agreed, a date was set, and buoyed by the idea of a detox, I dodged Two Bottle Sunday.

The next week we met at Gatwick, sipping water and exchanging what snippets of knowledge we'd gleaned. I'd googled it, but

Michael moves in different circles: 'Everybody goes', apparently. Seven days lay in store. The first three or four almost completely foodless, combined with treatments to cleanse the system. Then, very gradually, small portions, reintroduced to a healthy gut.

We ate our last meal as free men on the plane: three bizarre, small cold platelets of some sort of meat, nestling on a bed of green inconsequence.

The airport nearest to the clinic is Ljubljana, Slovenia, and we were greeted there by Jacob, our driver and clear winner of the year's Slovenian Man Who Looks Most Like John Belushi Award. He drove with a reckless abandon, using the speed limit as a rough lower guide to be acceded to only on the most acute of corners, steering the reassuringly chunky Merc haphazardly round the winding alpine roads while occasionally reaching under his seat to flip open and answer his old-school mobile. His breath came in a high-pitched whinny, catching the back of his throat as he barked instructions down the phone. Michael, prone to the odd slightly paranoid comic fantasy, was convinced we'd been kidnapped. Occasionally the car would lurch violently into oncoming traffic, most acutely at one point when, following an innocent enquiry about air conditioning, he attempted to remove his jacket. Jacob seemed to have little respect for his own life, his attention constantly split between his phone, the radio and the contents of his pockets. He only revealed what could be described as focus when he veered off the motorway, pulled into the services and sprinted off for fags.

It was with some relief that we were turfed out at the Mayr Clinic forecourt. A hotel-like detox centre set in glorious grounds next to a massive lake somewhere in Austria, cradled on either side by mountainous forest. (I'm no expert in Austrian geography and after the experiences I'm about to relate have very little interest in a return visit.)

Reception had a giddy, Mel Brooks vibe. A Germanic nurse, prone to sadistic giggling, detailed the philosophy of the Mayr, giving us a breakdown of potential treatments. This involved multiple inner sluicings, a range of massage options and something to do with metal. No booze. No sugar. No mobiles at dinner and very little mention of food. We were hungry upon arrival and assumed that, as the treatment didn't start till the next day, there would be a meal available that evening. When we asked, she repeated the word *meal*, laughed uproariously and said she would have a look in the kitchen. In the meantime she offered us a small thimble of orange gloop. Rather alarmingly, she didn't know what it was, only that it would *make everything better*. It didn't look like it would make everything better, it looked disgusting. It felt like a *Matrix* moment as we contemplated the gloop on the precipice of a foodless abyss. We downed it in one. It tasted OK, but it didn't make anything better.

Five minutes later she returned from the kitchen and said she could offer us a single apple, to share. We began to get the picture.

The connection between hotels and food is so hardwired that to be in a room without any food on offer was shocking. No minibar with a row of chocolate bars, no sugary shortbread by the teabags. At the Mayr, nothing. Just a tastefully austere bedroom, a television and a large window looking over the lake. No room service available, just the silence of the Alps echoing round your mind, and the rumbling of an empty stomach.

After waking up hungry, we both considered breakfast to be a tad confrontational. A small circle of stale bread, a thimble of broth and the tiniest of spoons to drink it with. The Mayr philosophy was to eat mindfully, in silence, to chew the bread and spoon the broth very slowly, contemplating the moment. The results over time would be weight loss, cleansing of the gut and a sharpened perception. We tried, we really did, but that first day the thing we were most mindful of was how small the bloody spoons were (in the moment), and how pitifully small the portions (in the moment). The guests were a diverse bunch united only by their regulation Mayr dressing gowns and immense personal income: elderly English gents muttering about the Azerbaijan 'situation', young impossibly blonde American girls exchanging Stanford gossip, jaded executives tending to damaged livers, and tables of heavily made-up, bejewelled mid-European women with unfeasible foreheads. Conversation was muted. We had arrived midway through the week. Day three of treatment was the worst by all accounts, the hunger pangs reaching such a crescendo that many, we were told, took to their bed in tears before emerging on day four full of energy, refreshed, anew. The waiters dispersed spelt bread, broth and an occasional egg. No drinks at table, water to be drunk half an hour after the meal.

The week settled into a pleasant enough formula. We joined the steady stream of confused hungry people in dressing gowns wandering the corridors, going into the wrong rooms, wandering out again, trying to make sure they were on time for the next treatment, which they didn't quite understand. I didn't do many treatments. I didn't want to strain Michael's generosity, and it had been established at my first consultation that I wasn't really a priority. The gloriously named Dr Spock examined me. He was a very thin, bespectacled gentleman, fascinated by intestinal function, who hovered round me, taking my blood pressure and pulse, and dispensing Epsom salts to facilitate bowel health and alkaline powders to recalibrate the body. 'Good. Very good,' he intoned. 'You seem in good health. No weight problems, good numbers. Mmm... yes... I have to ask: Why are you here?'

'I'm here with a mate, it's just a laugh for me if that's possible,' I replied. At this, Dr Spock noticeably relaxed. I told him I was a runner and all I really needed was direction to the nearest woods. I settled in to my low-calorie alpine jolly.

Running with no fuel was a tough one. The shock to my system was such that I could hardly run at all. When I set forth from the lobby on the second day, I was so hungry I had half a mind to run down the road to the sweet shop. Truth was, I didn't have the energy; 20 minutes was all I could muster. My legs felt completely empty, there was no fire in the hole, just a listless sensation that left me stalling roadside on an Austrian lay-by. What was I doing here? Was I weakening myself?

It wasn't all gloom at the Mayr, and the lack of food made you thankful for the smallest of mercies. Eleven a.m. was a particular highlight. As the hour approached, the word *bouillon* would ripple through the grounds. Pyjama-clad zombies would pop out of rooms and scurry down the corridor. Pretty soon the starved masses would be mustering with intent, chatting like extras on *The Great Escape*. As the clock struck, staff would arrive to deposit on the dining room table a very large silver container full of watery, flavoursome soup.

We'd grab our mugs en masse and dip in gratefully. Characters emerged. Scott introduced himself, I had seen him on the first morning, sneakily smoking on the balcony outside his room. He stood at about 5 foot 6, though I should perhaps say he slumped; I reckon there was at least another 2 inches in there somewhere. A lively spirit shone through his very open, immediately likeable, rounded face, offset by greying black hair shaped in a peculiar bowl cut. The accent was warm and conspiratorial but hard to place. Initially I thought South African, then I briefly settled on Austrian before eventually finding out it was Welsh. Turned out he'd been at the Mayr a month and was staying a further three to four months. *Voluntarily.* He managed five companies and couldn't trust himself to go home. The unspoken conclusion to this, of course, was that he'd never leave. I looked at him, slightly disturbed as he relayed his love of the bouillon, the friendly staff, beautiful grounds. Two days in, I couldn't wait to leave. Four months? 'So relaxing,' he said, 'I can chill out, get some peace.' At the same time, he pulsed with a barely restrained inner chaos. Every evening his room shook to the sounds of heavy thrash metal while he barked down the phone, presumably managing his companies. A man obviously addicted to stress but who couldn't handle it without ruining his body.

'Don't you just want to go home?' we asked.

'I know if I go home I'll revert back. It's all or nothing,' he declared.

'Well, welcome to nothing,' Michael laughed.

Another Mayr resident, Lizzie from the heartlands of Buckinghamshire, also took us into her confidence, confessing that she had been sneaking into the kitchen at night to steal food. She guiltily glanced left and right, relaying desperately tense 3 a.m. raids during which she had snaffled two pears and a cherry. She seemed completely unaware that she was paying for the experience and could leave at any time.

'But it's all about the weigh-in at the end of the week. If I don't lose five kilos in the first week my husband keeps me here for a second.' She looked on the verge of tears but laughed at the end of every sentence.

It was a tough experience.

The initial rather comic excitement at the total lack of food subsided, to be replaced by a nagging horror. I realised just how much I missed it. Not to eat it, but just knowing it was there. We are, I understood, cocooned by its constant availability. There were no biscuit tins nearby, no bread bins to cushion our existential angst. No crisps, nuts, fruit.

Afternoons were the hardest. The sensation of feeling hungry at four and knowing that all you've got to look forward to for the rest of the day is a cup of watery soup and a pair of thin yellowy crackers was crushing. Some people didn't even get crackers. The evening meal was tense. It was the main meal of the day and you never knew how much you'd get. Over the week it began to assume the character of an awards ceremony. At the stroke of six, the entire dining room looked left to the kitchen galley as waiters sprang forth, serving up individually tailored dishes according to stages of treatment. Some got soup and crackers, others just soup – and some lucky souls got a full meal, sparking much envy from the other diners, who might be at the same table. It was high comedy to see the wealthy being denied food by the charming but insistent serving staff; a class reversal moment of rich poignancy. It's a tough gig being a waiter at the Mayr. You spend all day dealing with clients/patients/customers who have paid to be denied food and who are now pleading for more food. Powerful people neutered by the unforgiving Austrian absolutism of doctor's orders.

'The doctor said I should be given more food.'

'I'm sorry, I haven't got that written down, sir.'

'But please,' comes the plea, 'I really need a cracker.'

'You can't have a cracker, sir, I'm afraid.'

'But the doctor...'

In our giddy state of hunger, and secure in the knowledge that crackers were forthcoming, it was all we could do not to cry laughing as pained expressions morphed into rictus grins masking utter desperation.

This all changed, of course, on the third day when Henry, a young Namibian waiter I had been getting on with, arrived at the table with crackers for Michael and none for me. Surely some mistake, I thought, as he placed the pathetically small bowl of watery soup on the table in front of my withering frame.

'Henry, come on, I must be getting crackers. I don't even need to be here. I'm healthy.'

Michael piped up in my defence. 'Paul should definitely have crackers. It's absurd. Look at him.'

Henry looked at me. I looked at Henry. He consulted his folder.

'I'll check at the kitchen,' he said, then turned on his heels and left.

I sat at the table. *I am here for a favour,* I thought. *I'm not a patient, I'm an assistant, sitting here starving in front of a cup of watery soup. Crackers are my right. I need the crackers.*

After two minutes watching Michael wolfing down his crackers, Henry returned from the kitchen. I couldn't see any crackers. He looked at me with clear eyes and an expression that was hard to read. There was a brief pause, into which my stomach fell, then he uttered the saddest sentence I have ever heard in my life.

'Mr Tonkinson doesn't get any crackers.'

It was a tragic moment laden with karma, given our earlier amusement. I sipped from my spoon, mourning my crackerless existence as Michael nearly choked laughing on his. 'You've got to just submit,' he said. 'Enjoy the madness. There's method in it.' Michael had been surprisingly resilient throughout (maybe he had more stores to draw on?!) but the food denial didn't seem to affect him as deeply. He pottered around making everybody laugh, much as he always does.

I found the hunger at times horrifying. Corridors echoed with the growling of empty stomachs. The hours limped by, it was hard to keep a grip on emotions, but there were moments when I glimpsed the sharpened perception that the Mayr philosophy promised. On the afternoon of the toughest third day, I was looking at the lake and swigging from a bottle of water. Water was the lifeblood of the Mayr, the only thing that was unlimited, kept in a fridge near the bouillon. It quickly became a habit to grab a bottle and swig constantly. Glancing towards the lake, weak in a state of angry acceptance but simultaneously intoxicated by the crystalline alpine air, I glimpsed the reflection of the lake as the light caught in the plastic of the bottle. I glugged heartily, the actual water merging with the reflection shimmering down my throat into a body seemingly full of water. I felt incredibly connected to that moment of watery joy. The longer I was there, the more such epiphanies seemed to happen. I was not only stopping to smell the flowers, I was seeing them, marvelling at the vividity of colour, their fragile beauty.

Was this the cure? Was I getting somewhere?

How hungry was I?

For goodness' sake: somebody give me a cracker!

We'd been told that the fourth day was the day when the Mayr treatment really clicked in. That was the tipping point at which the body, denied food and toxins, began to plug in to an inner pure supply of energy. How I waited! The third day was very hard, mentally more than anything. To be denied food when hungry puts you in a vulnerable place; it can get very challenging. But on the fourth day, it was true: I awoke reborn. My vision was clearer, all desperation had been replaced by an inner calm. Physically I was revitalised, so I strapped up and went for a run.

Turning right out of the hotel, I broke off into the vast, inviting forest that had been calling me all week. The contrast between day three and day four couldn't have been more pronounced. My limbs responded seamlessly to anything I asked of them, and I launched into the woods with a boundless energy, muscles fizzing with a clean vitality as my heart sang. The mountain was mine as I sallied up and down it for over two hours. What was happening? It was honestly one of the best runs of my life. Strong and untethered, I surged effortlessly up and down the trails, greedily chomping on the fresh forest air. The Mayr had performed its magic, my engine had been thoroughly sluiced, my spirit fired up. Crackerless – and crackers – I returned to base more goat than man.

My very being soared with the angels that evening, as I was reacquainted with an old friend: food.

We'd heard rumours of lamb on Sunday for certain patients, and wondered whether we might be in the picture. Michael's weight seemed a tad reluctant to depart its frame, but my treatment had been going well. I'd lost weight, was fighting fit ('numbers good') and I had crested the third day. Sitting down at table that evening, I dared to dream.

The clock struck six. Results time. I glanced left.

The waiters emerged. This time, Henry, grinning madly, plated me up a pyramid of proper food. Our previous confrontation melted away as I perused the vision before me. Lamb cutlet, three slices of carrot and a floret of broccoli. I gazed at it enraptured as Michael contemplated his crackers. He hadn't made the cut (of lamb); it was me who'd got the chop. Doctor hadn't given him lamb. No. *He* didn't have any lamb, no lamb for Michael, but Doctor had given me some, and it surrendered itself on the plate before me, glistening and fleshy, seeping with blood, floating in a sweet potato sauce. I cut off a small chunk and struggled to chew mindfully. My body imperceptibly slumped, the relief was tremendous. Home again. After three minutes, Michael could stand it no longer and retired to his room. I fell upon my meal with the gusto of Brian Blessed at an All You Can Eat Buffet.

At the weigh-in with Doctor Spock that Saturday morning, I discovered I had lost 9 kg (20 lb). Lizzie had lost 4 kg (9 lb), guaranteeing her another week. She's probably still there sipping bouillon with Scott, creeping round the kitchen with a pocketful of plums. Michael, to our amazement and the astonishment of Mayr medical professionals, had a late rush on the scales and lost a stone (6 kg/14 lb). The Mayr had done its work.

The week had taught me that I was stronger than I thought. It also told me that if you do stuff, just simply take action, you see results. Somewhere along the way, I had lost sight of this; I'd been overthinking everything. There's a lot to be said for pure will.

As the plane took off from Ljubljana, I wondered: *If I can go without food and drink like this, what else is possible?*

7

10 February. This is a journey into time

Back in London, the weight loss meant that I was noticeably faster on Tuesdays, and another week without booze had retilted my mental axis. February felt different this year. I wasn't just surrendering to it; some of January's fortitude had spilled over, and I'd reconnected with my sober self. It no longer felt like a tedious penance. Maybe, just maybe, at the age of 47, I could become one of those people who don't drink that much. You know the type. They smile breezily when you meet them by chance outside the Co-op, effortlessly remembering your name and the names of your kids while you're desperately fishing for clues as to their identity. ('So, what you been up to?') I'm not saying they don't have problems, but they seemingly don't live in a way that makes their problems worse. They've recently been camping, keep on top of admin, and look like they don't still take pleasure in dunking a whole packet of choc 'n' nut cookies in a pint of milk, demolishing the lot and in the process guaranteeing an episode of IBS the next morning.

I was close to joining the ranks of the perennially chirpy, the more-sober-than-not brigade. The final step was for me to commit to a proper goal. I was definitely doing the marathon, I just hadn't defined my terms. There was something I wanted from it, but at the minute I was flirting, circling it coquettishly. Luckily, an old friend popped up to serve as an intervention.

It was a Crouch End Tuesday and I had rambled down to Coffee Circus mid-morning to fire up the old synapses. Hunched over a desk I saw a familiar face, a friend from the comedy circuit, beavering away on his laptop. I'll call him Matthew, cos that's his name. After brief greetings I enquired as to what he was working on. 'It's a book about time,' he said, 'or rather, timelessness. I'm working on it for the attention of Brian Cox.'

Matthew's a gentle, thoughtful fella whose physical appearance occupies a territory that sits halfway between Max Headroom and Robert Kilroy-Silk. (Apologies for these shameful '80s references. The elderly will remember them fondly. For the young: that's what Google is for.) He's a science geek with a penchant for very long baths and getting stoned, and had retired from comedy some time ago to play the markets. My antennae were piqued; I was on the verge of an anecdote.

He launched in: 'Thing about time is this: it doesn't actually exist.' A bold opening, as the café clock chimed 11.30 a.m.

'There's only one moment. The eternal now. Never changing. Not time as such. It's a non-starter.'

I tentatively observed that when we do comedy we're booked to appear at a certain time to perform, and that when we do perform it tends to last for 20 minutes. He smiled the smile of the timeless when addressing the timebound. 'That's not time itself,' he chimed. 'That's a man-made device, a measuring technique. Time is graded change.' He sipped his flat white and took a deep breath before diving into a detailed, though rambling monologue on the nature of time, taking in the origins of the universe, Hawking, neutrinos, and the utter fluidity and non-measurability of the space–time continuum. I kept to myself the irony of how slow time seems to go while discussing the unreality of time itself. To be fair, he was extremely cogent and operating several stratospheres beyond my level of understanding. The time thing was relevant to me; I'd been thinking of nothing else. Eventually, after 12 minutes/three days/several decades, he asked me what I was up to.

'I'm training actually. I'm doing the London marathon in April.'

'Oh yes? What time do you hope to do it in?' he asked, spontaneously combusting with irony.

I hesitated for a second. It all felt a bit grand to share a most private ambition, but then I thought, *Why not? Someone's got to make a stand, if not for common sense, for the notion of time itself.* 'Anything under three hours. I'm aiming to beat three hours for the marathon this year.'

It was new and exciting to say it, a public commitment. Only meaningful to me, of course. To Matthew I was merely contemplating a morning's graded change – but *I* knew, or at least I had an idea what I was signing up for. By saying it out loud, by actually aiming for sub-3, I was saying: *I am willing to train harder than ever, to live and eat better than ever to become the fittest I have ever been.* It was a mighty challenge issued, a declaration to the universe.

If I was going to beat three hours, it would take everything.

Now, before we proceed, a caveat. I don't want to alienate anyone with this sub-3 talk. There'll be runners faster than this, there'll be runners slower. The sub-3 thing is a symbol. It's just the time that represented for me an all-out effort, given my circumstances. Most of us have jobs. I'd love to live for a few months in the Rift Valley, run twice a day living off a diet of altitude and mung beans, but I can't. I've got dogs to walk, a wife I want to talk to, and kids to feed, who hate mung beans.

For me, sub-3 meant the next step. A gauntlet that, if grabbed, would test me to the limit. If I got there, I knew I'd have gone beyond previous efforts. The great thing about the marathon is that one size fits all. There are no requirements to enter, no ability needed. It's a blank canvas: when we enter a marathon, we are writing a cheque to our future selves, and we get to cash it in over 26.2 miles.

For a first-time marathoner, to run the whole distance is a *mighty* achievement. If you commit to doing this, to running every step, the marathon can give you everything you want. Basically, just by signing up to a marathon, you've taken the first steps to momentous change.

In setting a time, we are negotiating with an unforgiving master, who will shred us all regardless. There is no escape, the marathon will take its pound of flesh. One woman's 02:55:00 is another man's 04:15:00. That's the beauty of it. In many ways, the longer it takes you, the fitter you have to be. Towards the end of the field we're looking at running for six hours. I can't imagine how tough that is and I know runners who've completed it in 02:45:00 but attempted to jog it in 05:00:00 and dropped out.

So, don't fixate on the time thing.

If sub-3 is where you're at, fine. If not, replace it with your own – 03:30:00, 04:00:00, 05:00:00, 06:00:00. Sub-3 had become a thing for me from when I was a young athlete. Looking back, I was looking for a personal sign that I had encountered and conquered something deep within myself; I just didn't know it then.

Psychologists are fond of the notion that the map is not the territory. The described experience as laid out is vastly different to the experience as lived. We feel the truth of this every day, in small experiences and large. Climb Mount Everest, write a book. Walk to the shops, write one. Words will struggle to accurately describe the reality of both experiences.

Every marathon is a glorious adventure in which the map definitely is not the territory. This year, the sub-3 goal cranked it up further.

I thought I was signing up for a race – a tough race, but nevertheless just a race. In fact, unwittingly I'd opened up a right Pandora's Box. In aiming for sub-3, I'd done more than fill out a race entry. I later realised that I had, in fact (cue foreboding music), rung the bell for the opening round of a fight with myself (music intensifies as chapter ends!).

Mile 10. Rotherhithe. Observations from the pack

Goal time – 01:07:20. Actual time – 01:06:56

Spaces have appeared now, between the runners, room to manoeuvre. All weaving has ceased. We are on our singular path, writing our own story. Some follow the blue line helpfully painted on the ground by the organisers. This is the shortest, most economical route round the course. For many runners this becomes a minor obsession, a security blanket, and they cling to it assiduously. I hop on the line where possible but try not to stress, I'm still chilling. I'm working now, there's no denying it, but as yet, there's no distress. It's an honest morning's labour.

The excitement from the start has faded; even the crowds lining the roads through Rotherhithe seem a tad distant. It's a slightly harsh section of the course, the glamour of London Town is a long way away. Every now and again all shouting will cease and you'll fall into a pocket of relative silence. I say relative. It's at times like this that you realise the sheer earthiness of the running experience. For a spectator at this stage it all looks fairly controlled; in the pack it's a sweaty, surging mass of wind. Breathing rates vary wildly in intensity and volume; towards the end of marathons, breathing always becomes laboured, but even at the beginning the default frequency is a high-pitched whinny for some, or a spectacular throat-chomping spittle fest. Some groan, some literally choo-choo like mini steam engines. One breath in, two out.

Codes of conduct are lax while running. Certain things happen that are frowned upon in polite society. Spitting, for instance, is a regular occurrence, often involuntarily. For some runners, it seems a natural consequence of breathing while in motion. They're like a faucet. You might find the odd snot jet being dispatched forcefully from a nostril. Farts emerge. As long as these are artfully directed, no offence is taken.

For some, flatulence occurs sporadically as a consequence of poor pre-race diet. Others seem to use it as an aid to acceleration. I was once caught behind a club mate during an intense 5k road race. With less than one kilometre to go, he sped up suddenly, shrilly farting on each of the next six strides. It appeared that he was trying to outrun his own gas. Either that or he'd discovered a new mode of jet propulsion. Whatever, it was an anal cacophony that signalled his victory and my defeat. I let him run on ahead, suddenly lacking all appetite for the chase.

Very, very rarely, you'll get a one-man band. A spitting, snot-jetting, farting force of nature. These runners, mostly men over 55, rarely apologise. To be fair, they've got a lot on.

Running styles also differ hugely and as the field spreads there's a chance to enjoy the multitude of forms on offer. Some run light and tall; others crab-like, like me, low to the ground, as if perched on an invisible stool. Every now and again you'll get a runner leaning backwards, arms windmilling as if they're being chased by imaginary demons. Over the race, most runners get lower, the body instinctively finding the most economical way to travel.

At this point, the pack is slowly but imperceptibly separating into different waves of runners. Some are steadily overtaking, others are sliding incrementally down the field. From above, this human ocean blends together; on the ground, engulfing others, not being swamped.

The race proper, the real drama has yet to begin, but seeds are being sown for all of us. It's a subtle process; some runners have already messed up. They've set off too fast, a fatal error. You can see it in their eyes as you pass – a fear really, an agonised realisation. Agony awaits us all, but if you're in trouble now, the next 16 miles are going to be truly awful. I've been there myself.

Today, I've settled into a pattern that's felt comfortable in the past. Drinking just a bit at every water station, and squeezing the rest on my quads, neck, my head and then, finally, my hamstrings. I've had my first gel and felt it descend to my legs, a gooey renewal of energy. Four more; I'll be doing one every 40 minutes. To the extent that you can call it at this idiotically early stage, I'm winning.

Which means I am ever so slowly overtaking.

8

Scarborough 1982, 5.30 a.m. Teenage kicks for free

Within weeks, running went the way of football and tennis: an activity denied. At home, under the new regime, pleasure was a bargaining tool, a privilege granted; it was less a place of peace, more a testing ground, a disciplinary arena. Absolutely a no-tolerance environment with every aspect of behaviour suddenly under the strictest supervision. The way you spoke, stood, ate, walked. To return from school was to fall into a series of jobs, a formalised ritual, a dance of sorts. The polishing of the shoes, tidying of the bedroom, ironing of the uniforms. Upon completion of the task, I would return to my station in the kitchen to ask if there were more jobs. At this point, the job would be inspected. Dependent on mood, and following inspection, either discipline would be dispensed or another job given out. If lucky, I would be dismissed to read in my room. If a bad mood was evident, I would be set an impossible task, such as finding an infinitesimally small object in the garden shed. After inevitable failure, consequences would be experienced, followed occasionally by the denial of food, then an early night – not that this guaranteed safety.

Kids adapt to circumstance and are very resilient. It was only when visiting other houses that I really noticed how absurd and cold my situation was. Normality appeared exotic. At meals, other families laughed and joked together. It wasn't an ordeal to be suffered in silence, bookended by jobs – the formal setting of the table, an assessment of manners while eating followed by the clearing of the table, washing and drying, then bed.

Looking back, one of the hardest things about life then was that it made it very hard to commit to sporting events. I was good at football. In fact, I'd been captain of the school team in my first year, but after several weekends of being denied the pass to go to matches on the morning of the game, it was less embarrassing and simpler just to stop playing. The same was true of running. This seemed to annoy her less than football for some reason, but even so, it was a privilege earned painstakingly during the week through tasks and compliance, as opposed to a right naturally permitted or encouraged. At times, after often trivial transgressions, running rights would be withdrawn and trainers confiscated (presumably harboured in the same cupboard that held the football boots). Having recently discovered a love for running, its denial was a perfectly weighted punishment. I had a manic urge, almost a need to run on my own, but no chance to do it. I ran my paper rounds, cycled to school, did PE, played playground football at dinnertime. These were activities that couldn't be stopped, but everything else was at her whim.

So, faced with this, and with the determination and courage of youth, I got up in the morning very early and ran in boots. It was, looking back, a perilous choice of action. I can't imagine the drama if I'd been discovered.

In the cupboard under the stairs, I had a pair of old army walking boots, which had been given to me by my grandparents. Because they were off the usual rota of shoes, they avoided the daily inspection and cleaning process. I figured if I could get hold of them, they'd be perfect; essential props for my bloody-minded 12-year-old self. The only question was: when could I get them? The only answer was: in the morning, before the paper round. That meant setting the alarm for 5 a.m., stealthily sneaking out of the bedroom, across the landing outside my parents' bedroom ever so softly, down the stairs gently, into the cupboard under the stairs, get the boots, tiptoe through the kitchen and out the back door, being extra careful to click it shut as quietly as possible. The whole escapade was like a burglary in reverse.

Once out, I'd creep out the front gate and set off into the dawn, released, free at last to rampage round the clifftop paths and gardens of the South Bay. The boots were heavier than trainers, of course, but added to the drama as I yomped merrily up hill and down dale. I also realised, even at that early age, that I'd feel the effects when I got my trainers back. I wouldn't have time to run far, just 30 minutes or so in the clean cool air of a coastal morning. Often, when returning home, I'd take the boots off and do some sprints barefoot on the putting green outside the clock tower, relishing the cool morning dew fizzing off my toes. It must have been an odd sight for early morning workers and, without doubt, it was a highly unusual activity for a young teenager.

Looking back at my 12-/13-/14-year-old self, I marvel at the clear-eyed determination of that slight figure drying his feet off on the park bench before jogging home. It was an incredibly risky thing to do. To rise at dawn and run in boots was a small win. In a life when so much was out of my hands, it represented a reclamation of power, a moment that was purely mine.

Back in the house, I'd snake my way back through the kitchen, return the boots to exactly the same place and tiptoe back to my bedroom. Twenty minutes or so later, I'd be feigning sleep and she'd march in and snap the curtains open. Five minutes later I'd be up and out again, running down to the shop for the paper round.

9

Crouch End. Dirty Burger. Richard gets behind the sub-3 goal

It had been a while since I'd seen dear old Richard. As 21st-century types often do, we'd been diarising with intent for weeks across a range of media platforms, but eventually it was a text pinging on my phone that sealed the deal, offering as it did a time and a place.

Dirty Burger. 1pm. And an exhortation: *Bring an appetite!*

It was a loaded invitation, both the location and the comment about appetite. He knew I was in training, that he was setting up a conflict. The meal would inevitably descend into a coded test of friendship, a battlefield of contrasting lifestyles, a struggle between the virtues of pleasure and unfettered hedonism versus the ethics of denial and athleticism.

It's not quite as simple as that, of course. Richard had worked way harder than me all his life. I'd fallen into stand-up straight from university, a peripatetic endeavour noticeable for its lengthy lie-ins, late nights and giddy highs. Of course, it's work of a kind – anyone who toils in the creative industries will know the ego-shredding demands – but still, from a distance, to the untrained eye, it's hard to differentiate it from just arsing about. Richard had gone a different route: he'd ascended the corporate ladder and knew what real discipline looked like. Sixty-hour working weeks, weekends networking in Geneva, agenda-saturated meals – and the dissolving of the business–pleasure boundary so that 20 years in, you didn't know which was which. All you knew was that you were really good at golf, and had rocketing blood pressure and a healthy property portfolio.

We sat down that Wednesday lunchtime at opposite ends of the work–income spectrum. He had nicked 45 minutes from his busy schedule to slum it; I'd been looking forward to it all week and was desperately scanning the prices.

'Well, it's got to be a dirty burger,' Richard insisted. 'We're in Dirty Burger. Dirty burger, crinkle-cut fries and a full fat Coke, I reckon.' The waiter wasn't even with us.

'I reckon I might go chicken, maybe even a salad.' I presented a casual honesty at the table, gently pushing his buttons.

'What?'

'Here, look, they do a Dirty Beet, a beetroot and fennel patty, with a bit of salad.' An offhand insouciance, calculated to enrage.

'I don't want to look. You're having beetroot at a Dirty Burger?'

Game on. 'Beetroot aids recovery. I ran eight miles this morning. It's perfect, actually.' Three unarguable factual statements.

'Beetroot aids recovery ... It's perfect actually.' Richard echoed. 'What's happened to you? You're acting like the love child of Mo Farah and Paula Radcliffe. What next? You gonna do a Mobot and dump in the corner?' If I were a teenager, I'd call that classic bantz. We weren't rowing, it was a continuation of the kitchen at my wife's 50th.

'I'm training for a marathon.'

'It's in April!'

'I know, but it all starts here. You need to eat right. I'm doing it right this time.'

'What do you mean, doing it right? You've always done it right, how can you possibly do it wrong? Set off from The Mall and run to Greenwich. How hard can it get? You just run with everyone else, like all the other lemmings, and then bore us by chasing up sponsorship.' This seemed a bit harsh – element of truth, though; the sponsorship's a tough ask.

The waiter, who had been hovering, pressed forward. 'Would you like some drinks before you order?'

Richard went first. 'I'll have a banana milkshake, please.'

'Tap water's fine for me, thank you.'

Richard swallowed down. 'Actually—' he glanced at his watch, sighing deeply as if in the presence of a great and possibly infectious idiocy, '— I've changed my mind. Can I have a beer?'

As the waiter sauntered off, Richard looked suddenly serious and leaned over the table, speaking in mock serious hushed tones. 'Do you want to borrow some money?'

'No, I'm fine.'

'Are you absolutely sure? I know comedy's difficult, especially how you do it.' (Low blow!) 'Honestly, I'll pay. It's on me.' He threw his arms wide open in invitation. 'Tuck in. Seriously. Indulge yourself.'

'It's not that.'

He leaned forward again, conspiratorially glancing left and right as he did so. 'Are we being watched by the security services? Is your life in danger?'

'You're annoying me now.'

'Nod twice if the answer's yes.'

'Please stop.'

'Is *beetroot* your safe word?'

'No.'

'Then why are you having tap water?'

'It's just hydration. It's the best thing.'

'Well, have a Coke at least, an orange juice, live a little.'

'Tsk. Very sugary. I'm trying to cut down on sugars. The thing is, I'm aiming for a sub 3-hour marathon. It's going to be super-tough. I'm going to have to give up some stuff, so... that's what I'm doing.'

'It's hard enough already, why ramp it up?'

He looked at me, genuinely forlorn. For a second, I thought he might up and leave. The opening rounds were over; it was time to get to the chase so we could eat as buddies.

I changed tack.

'How old are you?'

He garbled into his collar.

'Stop mumbling. Tell me your age.'

'Forty-eight.'

'OK. So... What's the aim here?'

'What do you mean?'

'Where does this go? The burgers, the booze, the drugs.'

Richard paused for a second. The waiter returned, placing the beer artfully in front of him. Richard's eyes followed the jug of water distrustfully as it took its watery place in the middle of the table. 'What do you mean, where does it go? We used to dance all night.'

'That's my point, it's not like we didn't do it. We did that for years. We used to dance all night and recover all week. Don't you ever tire of it? Don't you just want to call an end to it?'

'Actually, no. Not yet anyway.'

'Running makes you feel good, you know, on a purely physical level. Endorphins, in the brain. It's chemical. You'd love it. The feeling you get from a good run, they call it a runner's high.'

'I get the same buzz from meat.'

'But meat repeats on you. Running makes you feel better afterwards, all day. I'm telling you, it just works.'

'I worry about you. Where's the fun?'

'Are we ready for our orders?' the waitress interjected.

'Yes, thanks.' Richard cheered up momentarily. 'I'll go for the Dirty Burger special, crinkle-cut chips and some garlic bread.' He looked at me over the table with half a challenge and half a plead. It was as if he was reaching out, brandishing a 25-year-old baton of friendship.

'It's on me,' he intoned. 'Anything. Go for it.'

I didn't hesitate.

'I'll have the beetroot and fennel patty, please, salad on the side.'

Richard looked close to being sick.

'And the burger?' the waitress piped up.

'Yes, please, a burger,' he repeated in a monotone.

'How would you like it? Well done, medium...?'

'Rare, please.' Ever so slightly bristling, he handed the menu back before swivelling towards me. 'I want to see blood.'

10

Late February. Tuesday track. The voices, the voices

We are besieged by voices throughout our life. Every day our minds are at war as conflicting messages battle for supremacy. I was running more than ever that spring. I'd written a schedule and was following it. My body was slowly changing, I could feel it – but even so, testing moments piled up relentlessly. Not just Richard at Dirty Burger or the Roisin Conaty cake portal. They were everywhere.

My relationship with running was changing. I had begun to see it less as a purely physical activity, more as a psychological testing ground, a kinetic laboratory. Take, for instance, Tuesday training. As Gavin, Hoggy, Dom, Sarah and I ran long, punishing reps under the floodlights, my mind was like a boxing ring. In the red corner, a whip-cracking Anne Robinson-like taskmaster: *Push on! Dig deep! You are the weakest link!* In the blue corner, another voice was softer, holding out a metaphorical hash pipe. Call it my inner Snoop Dogg: *Chill out, Mr T, you've got nothing to prove. Enjoy yourself, homey.*

I guess we're talking about willpower here, and exercising it. When in pain, it's hard to justify or listen to the voice that says *Push on, do more,* but sometimes, I was beginning to realise, it's necessary. Anything difficult includes moments of discomfort; that's where growth happens. On a physical level, that's where muscles grow – the heart expands, the system adapts to differing physical demands – but it was obvious to me that I hadn't quite cracked the mental journey yet. In short, over time I'd established a way of life that subtly but constantly ran contrary to my best interests.

It's a truth well known that in life we know what we should do and we don't do it. We might look like we're giving it our best, but deep down, we know. This stuff goes deep, is embedded in us. It's simplistic to say this is good versus evil. To put on my psychologist's hat for a second, I think it's at least partly linked to the dominant voices that you heard when growing up. Was the encouragement that you received coming from a kind, loving place or a harsh, cold, judgemental one? If you associate striving with a lack of self-worth, it can seem more attractive to ease up – an act of rebellion, or even self-preservation. Who hasn't felt the relief at that moment of surrender amid great struggle, the realisation that all things will pass, that it's all irrelevant in the grander scheme of things? Does it really matter? We're grown-ups now, we can do what we want.

To be rude for a second, fuck it.

Historically, I had definitely favoured my inner Snoop. When faced with two choices, I had become very good at going easy on myself. I'd even extended this to fashion choices. Over the years I'd developed a penchant for velour lounge tracksuits, baggy T-shirts and phat trainers. In my mind, I was rolling a hip-hop/*Sopranos* vibe, though the point of reference for close friends was more *Golden Girls* meets *Brookside*. Spiritually I'd hurled a smidgeon of Buddhism into the mix: I had made peace with the world, I was in a state of not seeking, happy with less. I'd fashioned an existence that contained as little striving as possible. Perhaps it was age, but I felt I'd reached a settlement with life. Career-wise, everything was ticking over nicely. The gigs took care of themselves, I was travelling the world doing huge arenas with Michael, occasional TV popped up, the podcast grew steadily. Family life held its inevitable joys, and

I took my place happily within it. It felt like I had become that rare creature, a happy Dad, and I was absurdly grateful to be one. That's to say I saw my chief role in the theatre of life as essentially one of provider and protector: food, lifts, money. I was the frame and my kids were the picture. This was fine. At 47, I'd had my time in the sun – I'd hosted shows, suckled on the inflamed nipple of fame – and now I reclined comfortably in the bosom of home life, where I performed my duties happily. I was a velour-clad, mini-cab-driving, food-dispensing, mobile cash machine. Don't think it had all been easy; this had been a tumultuous journey with many idiotic and self-destructive episodes, but finally, family had become my raison d'être, the main creative endeavour. I noted with interest that even Snoop, in his mid-40s, had settled down.

And, on the whole, happiness had become for me a daily default setting, totally unconnected to any kind of worldly achievement. I found it everywhere: in the lolloping gait of my dog on a morning, my b-boy son spinning round on his head, my wife's voice. Other stuff as well, which some may find humdrum. Supermarkets, for instance. I love them. I think it's the proximity of all that food, and the variety of it. Honestly, I can get a bit emotional. You might find me smiling serenely by the cheese aisle, eyes glistening as I ponder the plethora of options. All this produce from all over the world! And all the people who made it possible: the growers and pickers and distributors, the thousands upon thousands of people who got together to fill this supermarket. What wondrousness is this! And now I'm here, standing in the queue; I refuse to use the customer-only tills because I know all the staff. I'm that guy. Out and about in Crouch End, I chat to everyone all the time, merrily surfing that line between chatty, lovely bloke and community irritant. I'm everyone's mate! Lollipop ladies, street characters, the homeless – I welcome them all. I find joy in the everyday. The Sufi mystic Rumi once said, *Comparison is the thief of joy*. I was all over that. I didn't lose a second to envy, I had burst through the societal matrix into a velour wonderland.

BUT.

Sometimes, just sometimes, a nagging sensation emerged. As I struggled up the hill, laden with shopping bags like a human buckaroo, I found myself wondering: *am I really being honest with myself?* While emptying the contents of the shopping into various cupboards, the thought occasionally popped up: *Am I really happy in the world or am I withdrawing from it for some reason?* Even the dogs seemed to be getting a bit bored with me, their looks accusatory, their black doleful eyes peering up at me with the suggestion that perhaps I was in fact living in a state of gentle despair? Had I packed up my toys and literally gone home? If so, was this an acceptable way to live? What gave me the right to pootle around Crouch End like Lord of the Manor at the age of 47? Did I perhaps have more to give?

Also, on a basic level, if I was so happy, why was I getting pissed all the time? What was the root of that weekly drowning in Bordeaux?

It's quite safe when nothing matters, isn't it? You're untouchable, really. It's a philosophy bordering on nihilism, surely the coward's route. It certainly seems to be the state of many failed romantics, people who've felt that too much mattered and who have been hurt. After all, it's only when you say something *does* matter that you make yourself vulnerable – because then it might not happen, or you might lose it.

For some reason that I didn't quite understand, I'd established to myself that I wanted to run a fast marathon. There was something it could give me that I didn't have already, it offered a meaning beyond itself. A chord had been struck, and it echoed insistently. Maybe for now, it was as simple as, it offered an excuse to be competitive again.

I think I also saw that the inner motivational voice doesn't have to be tied down to traumatic childhood feelings of never being good enough. Rather, it can be liberating, a stretch out into the world, an optimistic surge into an unknown future.

Late that February, I experienced a mini turning point. It was near the end of a long and arduous Tuesday track session. You'll know these can be fairly torturous for me. Usually I start off fine and then fade markedly near the end as legs begin to smart and my inner Snoop applies his logic. *Why push? What is this really all about?* Cannier runners gobble me up like Pac-Man as my form disintegrates. This particular night, with 250 metres to go on the last painful rep, I could see a long shadow of another runner, about 5 metres behind me to my right. Backlit as we were by the floodlights, it projected itself onto the grass at the side of the track, the monstrously long arms and legs reaching out to drag me down to its shadowy underworld, a place of defeat and darkness. It was a comically physical embodiment of the issues I'd been grappling with recently. If I hadn't been so tired, I'd have laughed at the blatant symbolism of it. Here I was, faced with a living, breathing incarnation of my doubt. I scurried on into the last bend. Would I surrender as usual? Slow down in relief? After all, it doesn't matter. This time, I didn't. I listened to a new friendly but insistent voice announcing itself: *There's more, you can be more.* I steeled myself and kicked into the last bend, forging into the pain, gasping desperately for air, my legs withering in a slurry of lactic acid as I sprinted into that unforgiving final minute.

The shadow behind me receded, vanquished, and I finished alone, exhausted but happy. For a moment I had *become more.* Just for a second, I'd won. It felt new, I felt free of something. Whatever this was, whatever this challenge asked of me, I was determined to meet it. Up to that point I had been training, but now I was a smidgeon more committed. That winter, I promised myself, I would take the long way round. On one level, I would have to. After all, the science of training for marathons is very simple: you're training your body to keep running at pace when it really doesn't want to. Feel bad, run faster. You have to set this in stone mentally and physically.

That night, as I checked social media, Roisin Conaty popped up on the timeline. It was one of those 'I've been fighting off a hangover all day' updates. February had claimed another victim. To be fair, she'd held off the booze longer than me, but her fall was brutal. The photo diary spoke of post-binge carnage: a full breakfast, paracetamol, tea and a duvet in front of the telly day. That second day of January seemed like a distant memory. What happened to the no booze year? What happened to being our very own best friend?

It was a reminder if one were needed. I'd have to be permanently vigilant to ward off my inner Snoop.

Mile 13. Wapping. Halfway but NOT

Goal time – 01:28:25. Actual time – 01:28:34

A significant threshold is breached: for the first time today, there is less distance to run than I have run already.

This is a good moment to check in with myself. On the face of it I'm still running smoothly. To look at me, you'd imagine I'm holding it together – but, make no mistake, tiredness is steadily encroaching. There's a sense of agitation building. A transaction is taking place between myself and the distance. I am deep into the effects of training here, this is what the last few months have been about, but the first half has still taken its toll. I haven't run 13 miles at this pace for a long time, never during a marathon. Payment has been extracted, that's inescapable. Still the plan is holding. I'm bang on pace. I've thought about this a lot, the time I want to reach 13 miles in. It's a fairly narrow window to get it right, to beat the three hours. Somewhere between 88, 89 minutes. Any slower and I wouldn't do it; any faster and I'd implode in the second half.

So as I cross the marker for Mile 13, I'm in uncharted territory, but timewise I should be able to do this, it seems fairly simple. In fact, I've established a small time cushion, just in case I slow down in the second half, which is inevitabe. This all appears fairly straightforward.

The only problem is, the marathon doesn't work like that. Seasoned marathoners will tell you, 13 miles is not the halfway point. In terms of facts, they are absolutely wrong. In terms of the mental and physical energy needed, they are awfully, absolutely right.

In defining 13 miles as being halfway through a marathon, you are making a category error. The real halfway point is 20 miles.

Why? Because, as I've come to learn, marathons are not primarily a physical experience. They are a mental, spiritual journey played out in physical form. I know, I know, but indulge me for a second.

The truth is, I've been flirting with you. The first section of the book has been funny in parts, serious in others. While hinting at the deep motivations that make the marathon attractive, it's mixed practical advice with showbiz anecdotes, for an essentially light tone.

Now it's time to get serious. In reality, the marathon is more than just a very fun thing to do; it is also, on another level, profoundly serious. Some would say that the more seriously you take it, the more fun you'll have. Isn't all meaningful fun an attempt, as Nietzsche once said, 'To regain the seriousness of a child at play'?

The marathon is a beautiful game to play with yourself. I honestly believe it can give you everything if you get it right. There are rules to learn, principles to apply, but crucially it is, above all, a mystery. As you cross the Mile 13 marker, down the second gel, sip the water and plunge into the second physical half of the run, the noise from the crowd shifts up a gear. They know you are approaching the very heart of the beast. They sense it in your ever so slightly truncated gait, the nagging weariness nibbling at your physical frame. And they know that *that* struggle is what the marathon is about; in fact, it's what they have come to see.

So dust down those inner voices, hunker down, gird your loins. *Prepare,* as Czech running legend Emil Zatopek famously once said, *to die a little.*

PART 2
The Monster: Miles 13–20

11

What's that coming over the hill?

When people say they are training for the marathon, what they really mean is that they are training for *the Wall*. The Wall *is* the marathon – and the success of any marathon you undertake will depend on your encounter with the Wall.

So what is this wall of which we speak?

Simply put, it is the point of the race at which things get really tiring. Google the term and you'll be confronted with some fairly anodyne descriptions. Apparently it occurs at 'some point between 16 and 22 miles'; it is the point at which 'glycogen stores in the liver and muscles become depleted', after which runners often 'shift focus from time goals to mere survival'. Well, let me tell you, it is a phenomenon that strikes fear into the heart of runners, who will often wince involuntarily when describing it, or gaze off rheumy-eyed into the distance like old men of the sea.

Some people think the Wall does not exist. These people have not run marathons.

Some people think that the Wall exists only if you don't train enough. These are people who have usually done so many marathons that they have gone weak in the mind. It's undoubtedly true that the harder you train, the better you are able to accommodate the Wall – but this doesn't mean it doesn't exist, it just means you have armed yourself for the fight. You won't beat it, but if you give it everything, you might possibly reach an accommodation with it.

How can I explain it to you? People talk about *hitting* the Wall. This makes it sound like a dynamic process. It's not. It's more of a slow melting of energy and resolve, an insidious immersion into fatigue until suddenly it is all around you, the very substance that you breathe. You're left feeling flattened by the Wall, clawing at it helplessly as it closes in around you.

I was discussing this at a party once with TV comic Russell Howard. (I don't spend all my time discussing running, it just popped up.) Now Russell's a sporty type, a buffed-up ball of feel-good energy, tenacious and skilful on the football pitch and a dexterous, considerate lover (I'm writing this drunk) – but when talk settled upon his previous year's marathon, a deathly pale swamped his face. *Never again,* he vowed. *It's hell on Earth.* Halfway through his second vodka and cranberry, he struck upon possibly the best description I've heard of the Wall: 'profound inertia, an overwhelming abyss'. (I know: great party chat!)

That's a fairly accurate summation. On a scientific level, hitting the Wall means running out of glycogen. Glycogen is the chemical that stores carbohydrates, which convert to the energy that will propel the muscles. You take it for granted when you've got it, but when stores run low, its usefulness becomes blindingly apparent. Running becomes extremely difficult, you might even question why you are running at all.

Mentally, this is extremely disconcerting, upsetting even. All defences are down and your mind is suddenly flooded by unresolved psychological issues. You may find yourself suddenly wanting to phone a distant relative to apologise for your behaviour at Christmas 10 years ago, or thinking of a long lost lover and the day it all ended. Some people weep for no reason. The strangers who had been urging you on from the roadside now appear to be berating you.

Obviously, the fitter you are, the less this affects you, but there is no escaping it. You *will* come up against the Wall. Watch the marathon on TV: even the elite athletes usually slow down at the end. Form changes, shoulders tighten. It's like they're on a treadmill that has been ramped up to a 15 per cent incline, and as a result they're having to work much harder to less effect. The expression in the eyes glazes over in deep pain. On some level their experience of themselves is being assaulted. It's ridiculously hard and shockingly painful. If you are of a sadistic bent and have time on your hands, YouTube 'Collapsed compilation marathon' for a catalogue of demented, demoralised runners in the final throes of a marathon. Bendy-legged contestants bizarrely hop, skip and slump to the floor as basic motor function fails. Many are reduced to physically crawling on all fours as the finishing line approaches. Some slide along walls in search of support. It is both a grotesque carnival of human endeavour and a window into our utter frailty. Zombie-like, the spirit marches on inside a body reduced to a shell devoid of all energy.

What demonic hell is this? you may ask. How does it feel to experience it?

I ran my first marathon as a fit footballer. I was 35, had recently returned to running after a long hiatus, and I approached the big day cocooned by my naivety. I knew it would be tough, but as I lined up, I saw it as just another long run. I'd run as far as 16 miles in training, my legs had a bit of bounce, my heart was sound – how tough could it be?

The first 16 miles did indeed pass without incident. It was all new to me – the crowds, the atmosphere, it was like running in the middle of a giddy party. Even at Miles 17, 18, I felt OK. Looking back, I was running way too fast. Pumped with adrenaline, I got carried away. I'd made all the rookie errors you could make: setting off too fast; no gels; not training enough in the first place. As the marker for Mile 20 crested by the side of the road, I was becoming aware of a profound and unquenchable thirst, the dryness of a thousand summer days invading my throat. The pain in my legs was, at the same time, inexorably spreading, clustering around the knees, exerting an ever-tightening vice-like squeeze. If that wasn't enough, with every step that I took, it felt like my thighs were being violently punched by imaginary assassins. My head sagged, suddenly heavy, lurching towards the floor. Mentally and physically I began to retreat inside myself. It was like I'd been mugged by an invisible, all-powerful enemy.

As my physical form deteriorated, all mental strength went with it. Runners suddenly began streaming past, of all shapes and sizes. I let them go. Time considerations had completely left my mind, along with any sense of meaning. The only thought became: *How am I going to get to the finish?* I kept running, just, but the pace was comically slow. Fancy-dress runners sailed on ahead of me. An old man dressed as Fred Flintstone sped past. A young blonde female Pied Piper skipped by. I waved them on. For some reason, in this first marathon I felt extremely benevolent to other runners; reduced to my essence, I was very loving towards them all. As they overtook me, I'd encourage them wholeheartedly, often receiving worried expressions in return.

My race, as such, was over. I was now in another experience. I'd passed through to a zone of pure survival, where I was also overwhelmed by a feeling of utter absurdity. *What was I doing? Why had I taken this on?* A man who must have been over 60 ran past me in a silver dress, carrying a wand. I laughed almost manically. What had happened? I was utterly exhausted but not at all miserable. There was something almost comforting in the pain. It was so excessive, I had no option but to totally surrender to it, to sink gleefully into this whole body fuzz. There's a deep joy in acceptance of profound fatigue. Especially as pace was no longer a factor. All I had to do was run, however slowly, just run. I can always do that. By this time I was grasping at the spectators for sweets of any kind, gratefully scoffing jelly babies or Haribos. Dignity had long since departed: I had swerved off to the side of the road, literally in the gutter, stumbling like a drunkard in a failed attempt to catch a night bus. I'd eat anything, such was my primal hunger for any energy source. It's a good job a young mother hadn't offered her breast; I'd have ended up suckling.

I was lost. Delirious. In love with everyone and everything. Destroyed. Addicted.

And when I finished, when the agony ended and I turned the corner into the sweet, sweet Mall and crossed the line in 03:31:53, I couldn't wait to do it again.

The following year saw a different, much more organised and, looking back, a vastly overconfident and vaguely idiotic Tonkinson warming up by the celebrity start line. This time I'd trained very hard with a few long runs in the 18–20 mile region. Sub-3 would be a cinch I reckoned. At 36, I felt in peak condition. After all, my hero Carlos Lopez had won the Olympics at 37. I was confident I'd be the first celebrity to cross the line. At the very least I was sure that first celebrity finisher was a nigh-on certainty. I'm talking about 2004 here, the celebrity running field was a tad niche at the time. Johnny Lee Miller was well known, Nell McAndrew had emerged, but as we lined up I reckoned I could have it. I was the surprise package. They didn't know my history, the years with Scarborough Harriers. I wasn't some new arriviste. I was the real deal.

Setting off dead on sub-3 pace, I went through 13 miles feeling chipper, exactly on target and with the delusion that I'd reached halfway. Having passed Johnny Lee Miller early on, First Celebrity status was surely in the bag. Surging through Canary Wharf, at around Mile 18, I still felt great. Then, hitting Mile 20, an old friend jumped on my back. It was an almost comic moment of realisation: a massive 'D'oh!' floated above my head in an invisible thought balloon. To trick me into doing another marathon, my mind had forgotten this torture. My form immediately shrank, shoulders hunched, stride shortened. It was at this moment that I also lost the race within a race for first celebrity. The very second that I got walled, Tony Audenshaw from bloody *Emmerdale* waltzed by, generously urging me to 'dig in'.

(He went on to finish in 03:00:06.) The slowing-down process was, if anything, even more dramatic than the previous year because I was falling from a loftier perch; I'd actually trained for this, done the long runs. But when urged to dig in, I found it impossible. It was like a complete obliteration of the will. An absolute surrender to my inner Snoop. Put simply, I had nothing to dig in with; the very concept was meaningless. There was no shovel to hand, no surface on which to gain purchase. I was utterly lost again, adrift.

To my credit, I still managed to run the whole way – but not through pride or bullishness. Many people around me were stopping to walk, but I just knew that if I succumbed, if I opted out and settled in, that sweet relief of walking would be so absolutely different and soporifically comforting there'd be no way back to the world of running and that would just extend the shame. So I ran, sort of, slowly, ever so slowly. From a distance you might not have seen it as running; it was more a surreal demented shuffle. I had begun swinging my arms vigorously in an attempt to leverage the legs and was loudly muttering to myself. 'Come on!' I said, as if addressing a stranger, 'move your legs.' My feelings for the other runners were affectionate but possibly not quite as positive as the previous year. It felt like more of a defeat this time. Like I said before, everyone has different levels. I'd earmarked sub-3 as extremely attainable. As a youth running for Scarborough Harriers, all the club members seemed to be in the 02:30:00, 02:45:00 region. Sub-3 was deemed an extremely achievable time, almost inevitable assuming basic fitness. It was the '80s then, life was tougher; up north, club runners were a hardy bunch, having to run huge distances daily in order to hunt for food. But still, this was a huge wake-up call.

I crossed the line in 03:09:42, after what I thought had been perfect preparation. A deep and wearying knowledge dawned – running sub-3 was going to be a massive struggle.

My next attempt on the sub-3 a few years later was the strangest of all. For some reason, despite the fact that I was undertrained, I still lined up confident. I didn't bother with the celebrity start that year, my hold on this status is tenuous. Instead I sought out the sub-3 pacer among the masses to drag me along to my goal time. Preparation had been chaotic; drinking seemed to have been the foundation that spring, topped up with the very occasional run of absolutely no meaningful length. Yet there I was, standing in the middle of the sub-3 brigade looking like I belonged, saying the right things, stretching in the sun.

What was I thinking? How did I have the effrontery to believe I could beat three hours? I can only attempt to explain it as a fanatical, deranged belief in some form of magic, a misguided sense of my uniqueness, manifesting itself in the notion that something utterly fantastic would happen on the day. From somewhere my body would remember what it is to be fit, and my incredible reserves of will, which we have already established do not exist, would let me summon the strength to do it. By an act of mental and physical wizardry, my twisted pre-race thought pattern had coalesced around the notion that I could somehow circumnavigate all rules of preparation and assume a different athletic form for the duration of the marathon. I also overestimated the benefits that four days without booze pre-race would bring.

Like a prize fool I set off with the pacer and felt fairly bushed as early as Mile 6. By Mile 9 I was hanging on for dear life and desperate to urinate. Later on in my running life I hatched a devilishly simple plan for this very situation, but during this marathon I was still hampered by basic notions of decency and social decorum. Capitulating to the needs of my bladder, I hopped into a portaloo and hurriedly released a jet yellow flag of surrender. The game was up. I hadn't just stopped for the toilet; symbolically I'd given up the ghost. Sub-3 was disappearing down the road, along with all hopes of any magic. Already knackered, I faced another 17 miles. The road through Canary Wharf was bedlam and I wombled down the middle of it gracelessly in a sullen stuttering gait. Rock bottom had been reached and I was utterly beached. Bereft, lost, angry, no benevolence bubbled forth this time. I was annoyed, irritated with myself, infuriated by this shoddy pretence of an attempt.

What was the point? Why was I wasting everyone's time?

I waddled on, adrift in pointless marathon rage. Not to be too crude, though it fits the mood, the crowd were getting on my tits. Their cries of encouragement fell hollow in my ears, ringing false – but only because I was false. I had betrayed the contract, disrespected the event. This isn't to say that every time you run a marathon you'll run your best time, but you owe it to yourself, surely, to run the best one you can. What I should have done, knowing that I hadn't trained enough, was to set off conservatively and marshal my energies. I could have played the game of damage limitation. Instead, by my foolhardy pace, I had guaranteed maximum damage. I'd added idiocy to undertraining, a lethal cocktail.

The marathon is a truth teller, it will always tell you where you are. That day it told me.

Two low points have become indelibly seared into the memory bank.

One occurred coming through India Docks at around Mile 20. I'd long abandoned any hopes of a decent time. Dignity itself had flown the coup, replaced with lingering self-directed shame and resentment at the very existence of life itself. It was a major pity party, and only I was invited; there was no guest list. Physically, I was in an almost vegetable state of simply putting one step in front of the other. I had passed the worst phase of the Wall. Now, like someone who'd been mugged on their way home, I was stumbling onwards in a mildly shocked state with a suitably vacant expression.

(Always keep plodding on. This gets you to the finish, your bags and eventually a place of warmth.)

I wasn't in a competitive mindset by this stage, but even so, vestiges of pride remained. Then a man passed me to my right.

I can see him now. A less athletic specimen it's hard to imagine. First off, he was big. Runners come in all shapes and sizes, tall and thin, short and stocky. This guy occupied the rare tall and stocky category. Perfectly fair enough, but annoying in the circumstances. Secondly, his clothing added to my sense of injury. I'm no snob when it comes to gear. For me, it's the less the merrier: shorts and a vest suffice; I prefer to run sockless if possible. But I won't judge you if you're a fan of the compression sock or heart-rate monitor. Each to his own, it's a broad church. Good luck to you and Godspeed. Check out this guy's garb: cut-off jeans, old school hi-tec trainers, a T-shirt advertising a beer festival – all topped off with a string jumper! And it gets worse. On his back he was carrying a rucksack and when I saw him he was on his mobile, chatting away in an accent that suggested he was from south of the river, 'Yes, bruv, I'm coming through the Docks ... I'll meet you in the pub 'bout 'alf two ... It's alright ashually, enjoyin' meself... Tell you what,' he laughed, 'I'm garrrsping for a fag.' I was being overtaken by a smoker! Was nothing sacred? This experience that was tearing me to bits seemed more of a social event to him. Just a cheap way of getting from Greenwich to the centre of town. Could I fall any further?

Turns out I could. This one makes me physically wince to recall.

Still reeling from the encounter with the running smoker, I wasn't in the best of moods coming down the Embankment. As well as my parlous mental state, I was getting very hot and absolutely starving by this point. The whole day had become nightmarish and I was receiving goodies from spectators almost grudgingly. All good humour had vanished, and I was projecting furiously outwards. Our thoughts are the world, are they not? My mind was rotten, and so I was an accident waiting to happen. I grabbed carelessly at a small hand in the crowd holding out a jelly baby, snatching and dropping it simultaneously in a weak parody of helplessness. I stopped immediately and began to gaze resentfully downwards at the jelly baby, which lay prostrate on the tarmac, red and glistening. I knew how hard it was going to be, in my condition, to reach down, pick it up off the ground, stand up and pop it in my mouth but I also knew how determined I was to do it. It was a moment of utter desperate desire. I needed that red jelly baby. The red jelly baby had become my sole focus. A second ago, I had had that red jelly baby in my hands. Now the distance between me and the red jelly baby seemed an unbridgeable chasm. But my legs were howling already, singing with pain, to bend them was to ramp up their torment. Emotions had reached a frenzied pitch. I emitted a low, angry growl in the direction of the red jelly baby. My next move was to swear very loudly at the jelly baby itself. Of course I wasn't really swearing at the red jelly baby, I was swearing at myself, my stupidity, my exhaustion – which I thoroughly deserved. At that moment the red jelly baby was no longer merely a red jelly baby. It was everything and everybody that had ever wronged me. In my rapidly fracturing logic, the red jelly baby had become a symbol of the entire world – a world that had conspired against me to deny me this red jelly baby with all its sugary goodness and, by extension, every good in life. Maybe because my feelings were so acute, I found myself using a word that is definitely beyond justification, and I shouted it fulsomely. Then my eyes scanned north from the red jelly baby, and I saw a pair of tiny little feet in the smallest of red buckled shoes. I looked up in horror.

I had just forcefully screamed the c-word in the direction of a five-year-old girl.

I apologised repeatedly and sincerely at the time, but I'd like to take this public opportunity to apologise again. I can still see her shocked face looking disbelievingly into mine as she recoiled in fear and confusion, sheltered by the cradling arms of her dad. That's not the behaviour you expect when you take your daughter down to the Embankment to watch people doing the marathon. *Yes*, you might have said, *let's go and cheer the runners on in their fancy dress! Take some sweets, the runners love them! It's a wonderful day. You'll love it. It'll make a great 'What I did at the weekend story' for the mat on Monday.* The mat story you don't want your daughter to tell is: *I went down to the Embankment and learned the c-word off a total stranger after offering him a jelly baby.* People shouldn't act like this. I was wrong and I'm truly sorry. I'd also like to extend my gratitude to the father in question for not punching me in the face. It was obvious he wanted to, and I sense the only reason he didn't was because he didn't want to compound the trauma that his poor daughter had already experienced that Sunday morning.

I was horrified. How far had I fallen? How bad could this day get?

I reached down, grabbed the jelly baby, stood up with a sigh of total resignation, stuffed it greedily in my mouth and continued on my lonely, desperate, trudging path, more beast than man.

The Wall had won again.

12

Why this is not a misery memoir

Just so you know, this could easily have been a marathon–misery memoir hybrid. I've got the source material and could lay it on thick if I fancied. There are many reasons why I'm not going to, some of which are generational. I've done all the therapy and I absolutely recognise the need to talk about our emotions, to share our experiences in order to help others and move on together, but I must say I do fall in with the *let's not wash our dirty linen in public* school of thought. I am of a relatively private persuasion and don't like to dredge up the past too often. I'm getting better, more open; it's a matter of generational progression, isn't it? My dad's generation were a fairly unexpressive bunch; his dad was wound tight as a drum and I can only guess at what it was that produced him. It's like a Russian doll of emotional repression. The tide is now moving in a different direction, and future generations will doubtless emote more easily, all boundaries between public and private dissolving entirely as we curate our lives for public consumption.

Overall, I see this as a positive development. It's good to be and feel connected, so I will be sharing, but within limits. For a start, some of the people concerned are still alive. On a very basic level, it's not fair. It's also painful to revisit elements of my youth. It's way more fun not to, and it's sort of missing the point. Whatever happened was only one element. To spend too much time in that area is to foreground it. After all, childhood consists of many experiences.

My childhood was playing on the beach, eating ice cream, Christmas mornings, hide and seek, playing army in the woods, the incredible excitement of girls. It was being cheeky to teachers, nicking sweets and heading rolled-up socks into baskets. It was bubblegum, jigsaws and apple scrumping, calling round to mates, mischief night, skateboarding, hanging around on roofs, dare-dare-double dare, breaking into disused houses, 15-a-side football in the street with tennis balls. The sheer fun and wildness of an '80s' kid. That was the life I had, that was the meat of it and that shaped me just as much as the other stuff.

It's just that overshadowing it, at home, was a feeling of dread, the constant awareness of danger.

Early childhood was fairly complicated in ways that don't really add much to the story. Suffice to say by the age of six, I was back with my dad in Scarborough after spending a year living with my mum at her mum's house in Aldbrough St John. Things hadn't worked out between Mum and Dad and, in the ensuing court case, Dad won custody, which meant a return to Scarborough. I saw this as a result, being crazy about Dad. To me he was a hero, a policeman, an old-fashioned bobby of the beat. Tough and funny, he would return from work every day, regaling me with tales from the fight against crime. Scarborough is where I'd always lived, it was great to reconnect with old mates on the street and to cap it all, when I got back, Dad had shelled out on a new bike. I couldn't have been happier riding up and down Newlands Park Grove, cock of the walk on my new Tomahawk, after a year's mysterious interlude at Grandma's house – which only helped rock up the cool points. The only fly in the ointment was Dad's new girlfriend, who shall remain nameless, possibly for legal reasons.

It quickly became apparent that she wasn't into kids.

Now, it's important to qualify this with a bit of context. We're talking about a different world here: the '80s were so unlike today it's akin to discussing life on Mars. The current child-centred parental philosophy was light years away. Indeed, it may have arisen in reaction to the culture we were all brought up in.

The aim back then was to train the kids to grow up and take their place in the world. There were rules to learn, ways to behave. Adults were in charge and had licence to tell you off at home, on the street or in school. Teachers routinely hit kids: usually nothing too serious, a clip round the ear or a slap on the leg. During gym lessons, the PE teacher would sometimes ask a kid to pick out a plimsoll for a smacking. Chalk was thrown, and the odd board duster or other missile would be lustily hurled in the direction of noisy pupils. On the whole, such methods served as fairly efficient aids to concentration and blended in with the general atmosphere of violence in the playground. What I mean is we got through lessons and, as far as I can remember, nobody got expelled. It was part of a brutal honesty underpinning the school environment, one that would be distasteful now. There was no idea of finding the potential in all pupils. Kids who were not as academically gifted as others were branded remedial and could often be seen pushing a wheelbarrow around while other students were in maths. Everyone knew their lives would be different. It wasn't all bad: they'd leave school at 16, get a job and be earning money before the rest of us; they were respected.

(While researching some sections of this book I discovered that a few of my peers ended up doing fairly lengthy jail terms for a variety of offences, but what I'm saying is, they were educated first.)

In that era, the notion of being a good parent wasn't the consideration; the point was to be a good kid. Now, of course, tables have turned, parents obsess about how events will impact on the emotional well-being of children. Kids are listened to, and nurtured. Encouragement in itself is almost the ultimate value. Progress.

The early '80s were different. You did wrong, you got punished. Simple. When Dad's new girlfriend moved in, I accepted her authority unquestioningly. Seeing instantly that she lacked any motherly warmth (even after they got married, she refused to be called Mum, forever referred to as Aunty), I adjusted my behaviour accordingly. To be fair, it can't have been easy for her, a younger woman coming into a house with my dad and me, a young boy who, I'm sure, could be fairly boisterous. A volcanic temper became quickly apparent, most heartily displayed when Dad was at work. Explosive and bluntly expressed, these outbursts left me physically shaken and my nerves shredded.

Life had changed.

This was combined, as I've previously mentioned, with an extensive raft of new rules and regulations. Failure to comply in any area could lead to the denial of food and freedom, or worse. Occasionally and bizarrely, I'd be given lines! It was all very disturbing; fairly soon I began literally to pray on the way back from school that she wouldn't be in. Shift patterns dictated happiness. When she was working, I could relax; when she wasn't, I was on high alert. Episodes of anger increased in intensity and frequency, becoming at times a daily occurrence. They became sewn into the fabric of life. On the walk home from school, I'd often find myself physically trembling. Inside, amid the chaos, I found a way to mentally disengage.

To be tough, or at least to appear tough, became the most important thing in my life. To fight back was unthinkable at the time so I resolved to take her on through non-resistance, passivity – she wouldn't win. Some inner core had to be protected, rendered unreachable. Her actions had to be seen to have little effect, falling upon a blank canvas.

So that was life between the ages of six and 15. And all of it would be run through with constant reminders of one's innate uselessness, reinforcements that you would never amount to anything. I remember one afternoon being given a sheet of paper and told to write down in detail what I was going to do with my life when I left school and was on the dole. It was a bizarre form of negative visualisation, geared up to prepare me for a life of inevitable failure.

Sometimes the patterns of life were so austere as to be comic, even at the time. There was laughter, thank God; where would I have been without it?

Over the years, it became routine to eat tea outside. The mum who didn't want to be called Mum rustled up a couple of sandwiches and I'd skip out to the garden. Banished and temporarily forgotten about. In summer this would be fine, idyllic even – it offered up a chance to relax, to assess the mood in the house, and time to work out how to play it on re-entry. As winter drew in, teatime wasn't so much fun. I'd often be sitting in my shorts in the dark, scoffing banana sandwiches on the steps. I've mentioned before how every house forms its own reality, its own way of doing things. To me, my life was normal.

Mum not Mum vacillated between controlling every hour you lived or, on a whim, chucking you out at nine in the morning for the whole day. How I yearned for a day pass! On those carefree wonderful days, I'd be the kid who had nowhere to go for dinner, scrounging round other people's houses or playing snooker in the front room while listening to other kids' parents whispering sotto voce, 'Doesn't he have a home to go to?' Truth is, at those moments I was thankful not to and preferred hunger to the alternative.

Tea outside in the winter was less than idyllic. One particular night, the absurdity of it all became starkly apparent. As darkness fell I found myself at the usual perch on the steps, tucking into a banana sandwich. That night had a bit of a nip to it; I remember the cold pinching at my legs, and after just a few minutes it started to snow. Relieved, I walked to the back door, assuming that, even given her wild nature, at this point I'd surely be welcomed into the safe haven of the warm kitchen. No dice. Instructed to wait outside while she was on the phone, I resettled on the stoop. For some reason that's hard to fathom in retrospect, I remember dissolving into hysterics at the wild injustice of the moment, the sheer ridiculousness of the scene as snowflakes fell upon the increasingly damp sandwiches.

So that's it. Shall we wipe our mouths, as I did that night, and move on?

I know that my story is not special. I've shared what I have for texture alone, and to reach out to those who have had similar experiences. The more you live, the more you realise the utter ubiquity of pain. As far as I can make out, most people who are alive have had an experience or set of experiences that mean life afterwards can never be the same. Some people, of course, have horrendous, indescribable experiences, beside which mine pale by comparison. My skirmish just happened to be the period between 1975 and the summer of 1985, with my Mum/not Mum. For others it's an accident, an attack, abuse, the loss of a relative. It's being humiliated by your boss, or a stranger pressing against you on the Tube. Trauma comes in many forms. The pool of pain in life is deep and touches us all. It is almost the central experience in life; to feel that deep sense of violation and powerlessness in the face of life's cruelty. A puncturing of the self, after which the terms of existence have to be recalibrated. A decision has to be made: given this new information, how can I live? What am I going to do with this? How can I move on? (And move on we must.) If you deal with it right, it can make you more compassionate, soften the heart, humanise others – but, like I said before, it's not the whole story. Life is wild and wonderful. We have the capacity to heal and grow and contribute and laugh and all the good stuff, but first we have to recognise: there's a lot of pain around.

Before we get too maudlin, it's important to get some perspective. It's fashionable, given the current state of geopolitics, to lose ourselves in predictions of catastrophe. Like most generations, we are fascinated by the end of days, but let us not forget, most of us are very lucky. Just to be born at this moment in history is to win the lottery of life. In terms of life expectancy, health and wealth outcomes, we have by any meaningful metric absolutely cracked it. Look around you, and marvel!

I'm writing this in a public library and yes, like many public services it's under siege and who knows how long it will last, but my goodness, it seems to be functioning pretty well at this moment. Students are on the upper deck, studying for what, I presume, is a future they think will happen. Loungers of all ages pootle round the lower decks, idly perusing literature and music. Toddlers are in the room next to me, singing heartily. Life is good here. I'm warm, next to a power point, the wheels on the bus are going round and round.

So however tempting it is at times, especially at its toughest moments, we must never complain about marathons. It is a choice freely taken, under no duress. Indeed, just the fact that we have marathons at all is a sign of a comfortable society. Having satisfied for the most part our need for food and warmth, we have energy to burn. Poor countries do not, on the whole, organise mass marathons. Similarly, they don't seem to spend too much time mountaineering or going bungee jumping; the normal stuff of life is drama enough.

We are saturated in luxury. In fact, I reckon part of the marathon's attraction for me and others is that it reduces us to a simpler, more natural state. A happier, childlike sense of motion.

One of the happiest, most inspiring people I ever met was Joseph, an old Kenyan guy who used to work at the petrol station near me in Stoke Newington in the late '90s. Over the years he would see me in various states of fatigue and disorientation as party habits slowly gave way to the rigours of child rearing, though occasionally overlapping. He was a constant; ever smiling, he brimmed with vigour and an unbridled optimism, underpinned by a deep, overflowing sense of religious faith and a profound love for seemingly every moment he'd been given on Earth.

'How are you today?' he would ask, already laughing as I entered the shop. 'It is a great day today.'

Now, Joseph was of the persuasion that every day was a great day by virtue of the fact that it was a day. (Hard to argue with ultimately.) Every time I saw him he would breathlessly enquire about the young kids. If they came into the shop, he would light up and speed round to our side of the counter, offering them sweets with wild abandon.

'Take anything! Take it! Anything! It is yours to have.' The kids' eyes would swivel with confusion as uninhibited Kenyan bonhomie rubbed up against the slightly more neurotic Stoke Newington parental culture. *Isn't he a nice man? Say: thank you, Joseph.*

Any weather was cause for celebration. The sun would obviously be greeted with salutations. But the rain also: 'The trees love the rain! They love it. The wind and the rain. Yes!' If I was on my own, he would shout, 'Say hello to the kids' and always, as I left, 'Enjoy yourself.'

Sometimes we'd get beyond the everyday interaction to a deeper level. He'd open up to me with tales of Kenya and his childhood. Often such tales of darkness would be interspersed with his usual greetings to other customers. He would break off from describing how he got the tribal scars on his face. 'They come for me in the morning, many men, they put vines in my face, stretch me out – Enjoy yourself! – I jump off a platform, it was very high, I cried for three days, then I never cried again – Say hello to the kids!'

If Joseph had known I was putting this energy into a marathon, he would have found it faintly ridiculous. Any energy not dispensed looking after the family was hard to fathom. He worked all the hours that God sent to put his kids through university, and he came from a culture where people did not run marathons for fun. If they could run, it was a money thing.

So, beneath the drama and the sacrifice, I am aware this is all a lovely game and we are lucky to play it.

And I'm sure Joseph would wish us all well. 'Enjoy yourself!' he would exhort. 'Say hello to the kids. The trees love the rain. Don't set off too fast, or it will be a disaster for you.'

And then he would laugh, because today is a happy day.

13

Happy talking, talking happy talk

People do all manner of things to feel better, I know. Trolling, paintballing, landscape gardening, sudoku, base jumping, darts. Life is multifarious, a many-splendoured thing. There is nothing wrong with harmless fun. It's only when hobbies tip over into obsession that you need to really have a look at them. Sometimes it can creep up on you. I was chatting to a dear friend recently about his debt problem. He was in a huge hole financially and detailed the horrendous and impossible numbers he was juggling with: the letters from various agencies, the escalating sense of panic. It was a desperate picture that he painted; life as he knew it seemed to be under threat.

What could he do? How to proceed? His eyes carried huge bags, his voice strained with an undercurrent of fear.

We went back to his house to strategise over a cup of tea, whereupon he ushered me into a room filled with board games that he'd purchased in the preceding two months, to the value of more than £3000. When I questioned him along the lines of *Is this the right time to be spending such sums on board games*, he said that he found them helpful in developing logical thinking and problem solving!

Sometimes we are too close to our lives to question our dysfunctional behaviours. Not only that, we won't listen to mates, what do they know? *These games are an investment in my family's future!*

At root, we just want to feel good without feeling awful immediately afterwards.

I suppose it was inevitable that, sooner or later, I was going to have some therapy in my life. The route was circuitous. Running shepherded me through my teens. Contact with Mum/not Mum ended when I was 15. After the inevitable divorce, Dad and I moved from Scarborough to Northallerton and with the move a huge weight left my shoulders. I could relax around the house and run whenever I wanted. The release of it! It felt like the shedding of skin. By this time, Dad had also started running. We would go on long Sunday runs together around the surrounding hamlets, coming home to a deliciously slow-cooked rabbit stew. (As a policeman, one of the perks of the job seemed to be a fresh supply of poached rabbits and hare supplied by fellow officers.)

It was, however, an odd time to move, as I was just starting my final year at secondary school. Most kids had sorted their peer groups by then, so it was tough to break through. That year I was Billy No Mates. In fact, even Billy ignored me. My one true friend was a silver-haired, deeply tanned, 54-year-old French teacher and running enthusiast, George Eden, who became my first running coach.

George was a wafer-thin, short-sighted member of Rotherham Harriers, with a marathon PB of 02:48:12. He ran with a high-stepping cadence in a completely committed manner that was slightly undercut by his thick, heavily rimmed black spectacles. Our eyes met across an empty field as we saw each other trotting round the school playing field at lunchtime. It was an electric moment. Standing there in our running shorts, we immediately recognised a mutual fanaticism. Very soon we were meeting up to criss-cross the country paths of the surrounding area, doing hill reps together and long Sunday runs while George regaled me with tales of the great Northern club athletes from his heyday. Olympians such as Ron Hill, Jim Alder, John Whetton, Alan Simpson. He lent me books on great athletes of the '60s and '70s: Gordon Pirie, Ron

Clarke, Jim Ryun. I devoured tales of Herb Elliot and his eccentric coach Percy Cerutty, doing hill reps on the sand dunes in Australia. Marathons were becoming increasingly popular for women at this time and I stayed up all night to marvel at Joan Benoit as she won the LA marathon from the front with her low scuttling style and white cap. I became obsessed with long-distance legends Grete Waitz and Ingrid Kristiansen, studying their training schedules in *Athletics Weekly*, applying their Nordic methods to the school cross-country circuit of North Yorkshire.

The year was packed with races. Cross-country and road in the winter, track in the summer. It was my golden era as an athlete, where I set all my personal bests, a perfect synergy of physical potential and mental commitment for a couple of years. George was my Percy Cerutty, an utterly inspirational figure, constantly imploring me to run to the front in local school races. *Burn 'em off*, he'd whisper in my ear as I jogged to the start line. *Run like an animal!* For a while I did, sprinting to the front of the field and ruthlessly cranking up the pace. I was faster than most kids at local school level, mainly because nobody else was training like a lunatic. George would scribble training schedules on old envelopes – twice-a-day sessions, hill reps, intervals, 50-mile weeks at the age of 16. He'd stand trackside, taking notes and logging progress. At night I'd do hundreds of press-ups and sit-ups in front of a massive Bruce Springsteen poster in my bedroom. The only problem was, despite my total commitment, I wasn't actually that fast (#awkward). I was swift for Northallerton standards, but once I ventured beyond the relatively narrow confines of the Hambleton and District area, my lack of basic speed was ruthlessly exposed.

One year I qualified to put on a pale blue vest and run for North Yorkshire schools in the Senior 3000 metres. This gave me the honour of competing in the Northern schools championships and a day spent travelling by coach all the way across to Liverpool to be thoroughly thrashed by whippet-thin Scousers and Lancastrians. Days like these eliminate possible futures that might be gathering weight in a teenager's mind. Distant dreams of Olympic glory were shattered under a clear blue sky. I was eighth in a field of eight, in the process being lapped by all but one of the other athletes. Evidently, I was no track man. My favoured terrain was tarmac, local road races in Yorkshire. I got PBs of 01:18:16 for a half marathon, sub-01:00:00 for 10 miles (in the same race) and 00:27:18 for 5 miles – all times I couldn't get anywhere near now. I was a tough taskmaster in those days. It doesn't take a degree in psychology to work out that I was, as Richard would say, on the run from something. The recent scarring from Scarborough was my fuel, and in races I was fiercely competitive, pushing myself without mercy, finishing completely broken.

When the fifth year ended, I moved up into the sixth form. Social groups realigned, and all the students who'd had no time for me the year before were suddenly interested. Running fell away, slowly but inexorably, and, it has to be said, life got incomparably better. I swam off into a stream of good luck; the fruit machine of life just seemed to click into place: jackpot!

The first magnificent thing that happened to me was that I got into Manchester University to study Drama. If you'd known me at the age of 17, you'd have been amazed by this. I was an extremely undramatic character. My life consisted of running, playing pool and underage drinking. In lessons, although fairly bright, I was a very disruptive influence, walking out when I fancied it, harassing teachers with prank phone calls, hiding in cupboards during lessons. English was a particular 'doss'. At one stage I remember a poor girl crying during class because my antics were ruining her education; that was around the stage my teacher described me as 'not a serious candidate'. Purely on a whim and probably in an attempt to impress girls, I auditioned for and got the lead role in the school production of Francis Beaumont's 17th-century play, *Knight of the Burning Pestle.* That Christmas I took to the stage as Rafe and, to the amazement of my peers and myself, stormed it. It was a giddy sensation, to be onstage, gaining huge laughs – incredibly addictive. Rather late in the day, in terms of university applications, I pivoted from PE at Loughborough to Drama at Manchester, a tough course to get on. I lied horrendously at my interview, fabricating an obsession for theatre that involved writing numerous reviews for the school magazine. Absolute nonsense. I'd literally never been to see a play, there was no school magazine. Still, it was convincing enough to put me in the frame for a place. That in itself was the spur that encouraged me to work harder. Somehow I scraped two Bs and a D at A level (English Lit, Modern History and Economics) and at the end of the summer I'd been accepted in to Manchester University through the clearing process.

Manchester changed everything for me. Life, as I came to know it, started. I found comedy, a wife, a set of mates that carry me to this day – all from that stunningly fun three years.

I also hit Manchester at exactly the same time Chicago house did. It was the glory days of the Haçienda, Man Alive, Konspiracy, PSV – a joyous explosion of dance hall mayhem in which I gleefully participated.

I was away.

It was only when the idea of kids was broached that I thought therapy might be an idea. By then I was living in King's Cross with a large group of reprobates who'd come down from Manchester and scorched through the late '80s, early '90s in a blaze of hedonistic abandon. It was a blessed generation. As well as the marvellous house music coincidence, we were the last wave to get higher education paid for and also perfectly placed to get some property just before the housing market exploded. Then New Labour landed and things could only get better. I know, ridiculously fortunate. Not only that, but I hit the comedy boom in London in the early '90s. Comedy clubs were mushrooming round London and the country.

Anyone with an iota of talent was immediately plugged into a vast array of gigs and what felt like bundles of cash.

My ascent was swift. In 1992 I won the Hackney Empire New Act of the Year Award. This led to me being given a TV show to co-host with another bright young prospect, Miranda Sawyer (now an esteemed author and *Observer* columnist). The show was called *Raw Soup*, a messy but fun music comedy show on Carlton filmed in deepest Deptford, South London, 'Live from Albany Empire'. It was produced by Miles Ross (Jonathan's brother) and we had a right laugh introducing bands like Blur, Naughty By Nature and Jamiroquai to an often quite edgy urban crowd.

Within a couple of years, I was lording it round Soho like Tony Soprano in the latest casual sports garb. The contrast with my life in Yorkshire couldn't have been more pronounced. Several years previously I'd been doing a paper round, now I was awash in London sophistication, dipping panettone in coffee, hopping into taxis left, right and centre, doing stand-up on the TV.

At this point in my life it has to be said that running was the last thing on my mind. Identity had shifted, comedy was everything now. The focus was on cracking it: gigs, writing, auditions gave me structure, instead of races. I was testing myself in the more subjective realm of the media.

Yet again, fortune shone. It was a time when lots of new shows were being made. Magazine-style shows. These shows were looking for new faces and my rather goofy face fit.

From *Raw Soup* I picked up a gig hosting *The Sunday Show* on BBC2, another live show, which launched the careers of Peter Kay and Dennis Pennis. It was an incredibly intense experience, bordering on panic. A weekly bungee jump into a chaotic hour that could end up anywhere. A Sunday morning post-hangover, jolting, wake-up call for both the audience and most of the production staff who'd regularly find themselves at the Haçienda the night before.

After *The Sunday Show* I drifted into perhaps my happiest time on television: *MTV Hot*, a daily show that I wrote and appeared in, in 1997. An absolute scream; I was a supercool Euro VJ! It was pre-Russell Brand MTV when nobody was really paying attention, and as a result you had unlimited freedom. The crew was just me, writer David Hales and producer John Deol. We basically took the news of the day and spun it however we wanted. Characters developed, stupidity was unconfined. It was written and performed on the day, a very pure set-up in a simple white studio with a fixed camera. Pre-internet. Lovely. From there, I moved to a fairly disastrous but fun Channel 4 show, *Dicing With Debt*, where students had the chance to write off their student debt. (We ended up being scheduled directly opposite a new show on BBC Two hosted by Anne Robinson. It turned out, we were the weakest link.) Shortly after that I ended up getting a gig I'd craved for a while, *The Big Breakfast*. One of the biggest gigs on television at the time, the Channel 4 daily, live, early morning show. They don't make shows like this anymore, mainly because they are too expensive. I caught the last of it, really, taking over from Johnny Vaughan. Life had changed yet again. A car would be peeping outside my house at 3.30 a.m., we'd drive in and rehearse. At 6.30 in the morning, I'd be interviewing Coolio or, on one occasion, arm-wrestling Pamela Anderson. It was intense, white-hot fun. And all, or most of this, before I was 30.

Looking back now, a lot of this feels like it happened to a different person. They say that physically our cells replicate every seven years. That means there have been three replications since then, three transformations on a molecular level. Am I looking at a happy person swanning around Duffer of St George with his personal stylist, who's way more stylish than he is? Not particularly. I'm acting a role really, but it's all a bit of a reach, I'm not that guy. At root, I'm feeling a bit stupid, dislocated. Maybe it's just that I was too young to appreciate it properly.

➤Thornton-le-Dale, 1970 at my grandparents' house. First photo. Just… about… walking. Though I've finished marathons since in worse shape.

❯The same summer I believe. Up and about now – what are you looking at?

➤Scarborough, 1978. By the age of eight I was a fully fledged gang member. *The Beano* gang. We'd meet in the garage behind me. This is my Dennis the Menace impression.

◄ Scarborough Beach, 1983. A trophy! First under 15 and second overall to the guy on my right, whose higher status is reflected in the quality of his jacket – and badges!

▼ *Sunday Show*, 1998. Donna McPhail, Kevin Eldon and Jenny Ross. The *Sunday Show* was recorded live in Manchester – a great laugh. Hangover telly for the audience at home and often the presenters. Hard to say whether this photo is taken before or after the recording.

▲ My first coach, the glorious George Eden – sprinting for the line at the end of a local road race at the age of 62. Note the perfect form, relaxed upper body, no tension in his face or neck.

Paul Tonkinson

◄MTV Hot was very enjoyable. I loved being a Euro VJ! Here is my Euro VJ promotional material.

▼Manchester University gave me the chance to take risks and find my voice. Here, in a self-penned studio piece, I am about to strangle my fellow performer, Ewan Moar, in the name of art.

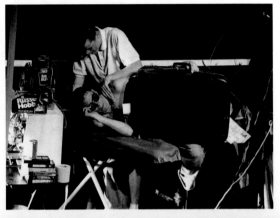

▼Here's the *Big Breakfast* team arriving at The Brit Awards, 2000. My co-presenters Amanda Byram and Donna Air shamelessly work the camera. I can't seem to find it.

➤➤I ran sporadically throughout the 90s... Here's me looking to get a quick start at one race and sprinting to the line in another. (The Hampstead 10k.) In fact the young spectator seems to be standing to attention, such is his awe.

➤You meet many different types running marathons. Here's me and my old pal (never met him), fellow author Jeffrey Archer, who's about to make a grab for that fella's watch.

> ➤ Near the finish of the same marathon. All the signs are there. The thousand-mile stare; I can barely lift my feet; bleeding nipples. I've been comprehensively 'walled'.

> ➤ Where's Pauly? See if you can spot me in this picture – winner gets a copy of this very book, which presumably by this stage you've already bought.

◄Methley Church. 31 January 1998. Just married. I'm in bits, having been a hot teary mess during the service. My wife Rachel is so happy she's about to eat my carnation.

▼Crouch End 10k, 2006. Rachel and I are coming to the finish of a local fun run. It can be stressful running as a couple. You'll notice, to keep the peace, I'm half a step behind.

▲How cute is this? Stretching pre-race, 2004. George is checking the correct way of doing things. Bonnie's arms are so short she seems to be headbutting the wall.

▲Post marathon, 2007. Bonnie, my little button. She smiles for the camera charmingly, I gaze on adoringly. All the time, she's making a discreet grab for the medal.

▲ Kosovo, 2003. In my natural habitat, entertaining the troops. The lads seem to be enjoying their cans as a prelude to chucking them in my direction.

▲ Just For Laughs, Montreal. Just got onstage at this prestige gig, although it seems something exciting has just happened off it!

◄ The master of positive self-talk. The very inspirational Gavin Evans holds forth pre-race as clubmates cluster.

▼ Here we have a classic Tonkinson sprint finish. Grit your teeth, lower your head, flail your arms around. Let anyone watching be in no doubt. I am trying, damn you, I am trying!

▼ Heathside Club Championship, 5000m. Where I'm happiest, a midweek tear up under the floodlights. Lovely. I'm about to launch my mid-race surge, to second last.

◄ Wimbledon with 'The Mac'. A break in play, and looks like we're making the best of the opportunity to catch up.

▼ Cuba, 2017. This is the very moment my eldest son, George, 18, realised the implications of an all-inclusive holiday. Bring on the cocktails and unlimited lattes!

◄ The podcast is simple – we run, we chat while we run, we record it. Here's myself and Rob Deering with the delightful Bryony Gordon looking like excitable cast members of a musical set in McDonald's.

▼ London Marathon. The sub-3 attempt, 2017. We pose for the media pre-race while exchanging mysterious messages behind our backs. 'Feel bad – run faster!'

▲ A podcast with the force of nature Vassos Alexander. Photo taken post record. My mouth is agape, greedily sucking in air with the effort of keeping up with him.

◄ My star, youngest son, Rudy and I after my big push for the sub-3. I'm physically shrunken by the effort, though this is exacerbated by Rudy standing on his tiptoes.

I took it too seriously to enjoy it. Now I've got a few years on the clock, I can see that showbiz becomes fun only when you see it for what it is – a gloriously ephemeral distraction, an essentially light activity. I thought it meant something, when the joy of it, especially in light entertainment, is that it doesn't – or, at least, doesn't try to. The clue's in the title. To survive, you cannot see every day as some kind of make-or-break ordeal. The usual demons beset me, familiar cycles of self-destruction followed by rebuild, which plague most of us to one degree or another. Bad choices in the fuelling department led to chronically stressed states of mind, which is something you don't need when it's live telly and you've got a TV camera swooping towards you and a director in your ear: *Camera coming to you in 5, 4, 3 ... relax ... 2 ... you're on 1 ... Have fun!*

Looking back, I wasn't spending enough time in supermarkets.

Still, I was holding it together (just). I had a great set of old mates with whom I'd raved through the early '90s and who remain close to this day. Most importantly, I was in a steady relationship with an absolute diamond, dear Ra, my rock, comic muse and angel wrapped in a lovely Northern package.

I'd known Ra for years; she was part of a large swirling group of mates who collected around a couple of chaotic flats in King's Cross during the early '90s. Over time, the relationship just seemed to creep up on us. I found her presence round the flat strangely calming and comic; something in the tone of her voice made me very happy, we laughed a lot. At warehouse raves on a weekend, it turned out she was just the right size to pick up and twirl around a bit. Not only that, if it was possible to make the situation better, when we all got home at the end of the night and were chilling out, being from Yorkshire, she made a cracking cup of tea. She also had a face like the moon and the softest of skin. To be alone with her was to arrive at a place I'd never known existed.

What can I say? It was love.

One summer's morning, completely unplanned, I experienced a rare but blinding moment of clarity. Before I knew it, I was running – yes, running – to Tiffany's to buy an engagement ring that I could not afford. A week later, on a trip away, I nervously pushed the small box in her direction and asked her if 'she fancied it'.

Once we'd established what I was actually asking, it turned out that she did.

We got married on a clear January morning in St Oswald's Church, Methley, West Yorkshire, surrounded by family and loads of mates up on a coach from London. I was a hot teary mess, shattered with happiness. The next day we flew off to the Maldives on honeymoon and that night you'd have found me at the bar, weeping again. I couldn't believe such joy was possible, that it would enter into my life.

It was on.

After the chaos of my childhood, something that I had fervently hoped for but found impossible to imagine: that most incredible of experiences, a 'normal' life.

Marriage, kids, the whole caboodle.

This brought up a few issues. I was connected enough to identify that cycles in life have a tendency to repeat if you don't understand them. I was absolutely determined not to pass on any of my childhood drama in the form of violence. It had to end with me so, as we prepared for the birth of our first kid, George, I hesitantly reached out, made the call and, for the first time, sat down in front of a trained professional.

If you've never had therapy before, I recommend it. I honestly don't know if it's the full answer, but it sends you on your way to one. At first, it's incredible. What blessed relief to sit down and offload, to be listened to by a professional who has no stake in your words but only a desire to help! It's like a modern confessional.

My first therapist was an NLP practitioner called Martin Weaver, a gentle, intelligent soul who took me into his small upstairs room in Chiswick, sat me down in his sumptuous leather chair and listened without judgement as I spilled my privileged guts all over the carpet while sporadically reaching for tissues. Let's face it, most of us are only four glasses of wine away from telling everybody everything. This had been building up for years and he got the full package. *Let me tell you about my life and all the stuff and why I'm like what I am like.*

What I got from NLP is tactics for life. It taught me how to reframe situations. Instead of being entirely at the whim of reality, I learned to take control, tilt the axis and see things from a different perspective. In terms of childhood trauma, we worked on timelines, visualising life as a long line and putting past events way back in the past where they belong, as opposed to carrying them round in the present. We reimagined scenarios from the past, changed the visuals, gained control over the memories a bit more. I learned to take a beat before self-sabotaging behaviour and ask: *What is this for?* (This is a useful question to ask if you ever find yourself smashing open a wine bottle with a hammer because you can't find the corkscrew. You might take a moment to think, *Why am I swearing at the bottle? Why am I caked in sweat and fizzing with rage?* Just an example.) He was also very good on changing states. If you find yourself in a massively stressed state, you can always just recognise it and change it. (You might find yourself on live television during a debate and thinking you're going to die of panic before you get a chance to speak, literally staring at your feet, waiting for your heart to burst through your chest. You could then reframe that chilling existential primal fear, call it a natural excitement, take a few deep breaths, physically force yourself to laugh a bit – and smile; after all, it's just a bit of TV.)

It was very useful stuff. I miss that room and occasionally, even now, return there to its practical, enlightening wisdom. Thank you, Martin.

NLP was great, and I learned some effective methods. It was also a gateway to more therapy and for the next 10 years or so, when I was sinking into panic or going a bit off the rails, I found myself in various and different chairs.

One therapist did my head in because he was always late. He was a more traditionalist, *talk it all out* kind of fella, but I found his constant tardiness a wind-up. Was it Gore Vidal who described being late as an act of violence? I'm sure any therapists out there would say I'm overreacting, but come on, healers, buy a watch! This guy would rock up 10 minutes late in full bike leathers and helmet, march across the floor to a side room and disappear for another three to four minutes. Finally, he'd emerge fresh-faced and then insist I pay him before the session started. What form of fresh nonsense is this? Payment in therapy is an odd moment already. After an hour of psychologically eviscerating yourself in front of a total stranger, he or she gestures rather mechanically towards the clock and you rise unsteadily to your feet, brush tears and snot off your shirt, reach into your pocket and say: 'How much?' It's a tawdry, transactional end to what has often been a life-changing hour with many breakthroughs. Impossible to put a price on it. In this case the price was £70, paid up front, after starting late (!?), and my major breakthrough was the realisation that I needed a new therapist as quickly as possible. Very soon he was on his bike. (Sorry, I couldn't resist.)

My next experience of therapy happened in Manchester. I'd accepted a job hosting a morning radio show for the recently launched XFM. The show was brilliant, to wake the area up was a privilege; we chatted to big stars – the likes of Rio Ferdinand and Noel Gallagher – and took calls from the very funny locals, who were a constant delight. It was, without doubt, the most fun I'd ever had in radio. The only problem was off the park, as they say in football, when the show ended.

The job involved working and living away from the family from Monday to Friday. For the first few weeks I was fine; that old Manchester house music sense memory kicked in, and I gallivanted round the old haunts in gleeful abandon. It felt like being 20 again. The only thing was that I wasn't 20, I was 35, and very soon I found myself missing home terribly.

Every week I'd leave the house on Sunday evening. Little Rudy, the youngest, was three at the time, and he'd be bawling his eyes out as I set off for Manchester. 'Why does Daddy have to go?'

Every week the question became harder to answer.

Professional obligations finished at about 10.30, leaving the rest of the day free. I was away from home with nothing to do. Other people would have played this differently; it was, after all, an opportunity for self-improvement. Released from the exhausting rigours of a young family, I had the chance to do all that stuff I wanted to do – get fit, work on the novel, learn a language, play piano. Alas, it was a test of my inner resources that I failed miserably. I am, above all, a social creature. I need people and, more importantly, my family. When on my own, I just can't find any meaning. Standing at the M&S checkout with a meal for one left me completely hollowed out. It wasn't long before booze started calling me during the afternoon. Standards quickly began to dip around basic hygiene, living conditions. As they say up north, I couldn't see the point in owt!

Luckily enough I had the nous to reach out, and found myself in the office of a very gifted, gentle lifesaver of a man called Peter, a gestalt therapist. Gestalt therapy is a German method of therapy, quite intense and physical. It wasn't just talking, which is why I liked it. There's a bit of role play; you might find yourself shouting at a cushion or having a conversation with someone from your past (in the form of a chair) in an effort to understand their viewpoint (swapping chairs while doing so). Peter was a brilliant therapist. Gestalt practitioners are very active, changing states during the session to physically reflect the changing subject matter and/or mood. He would slump, suddenly bolt up straight or just sit there, absolutely blank, a wonderfully pure embodied presence, amazing to experience. Like Martin before, he talked about different voices in our minds, and connected them to physical states. In order to heal, to fully move on, you had to listen to these voices, understand their root and incorporate them into your daily life.

I had two wildly contrasting voices pulling at me. The family side, the pull from home, battling with the hedonistic, self-destructive impulse. It sounds too literal, but I could feel my body almost changing as I drove up to Manchester and home life faded. Somewhere around Birmingham, I'd start to get a sort of pre-clubbing agitation. By the time I hit Manchester I'd be frothing at the mouth to 'have it!'

What Peter made clear was that both voices had my interests at heart, both wanted the best for me. I had to find a way of life which listened to both. What also became clear very quickly was that this life could only happen at home in London. I made arrangements to return as soon as possible.

I got a lot out of my time sitting with Peter in his room in Manchester; he taught me a lot. As with Martin, I extend my gratitude and wish him all the best.

It was around this time, when I returned to London, that running returned on a more regular basis. It had been teasing me on and off for years, that pure, simple medicine that never failed. An old impulse would grab me, and I'd be out of the door before I could stop myself. Every run would leave me centred, serene, suffused with a deep calmness – but for some reason I didn't jump back in wholeheartedly. I reckon it was because my peak years as a runner had been so all-consuming, so obviously a reaction to business buried deep. In my mind I associated running with relentlessly masochistic states and extreme competition. Nevertheless, slowly it returned, becoming a semi-regular feature. The comedy circuit had a few runners around, and I'd drop in on them from time to time. Rob Deering lived close to me and, as I mentioned earlier, we began to run in the woods. In time, the running took over from the therapy. Part of this was a matter of finance, part was that feeling of utter futility you get on the way to a therapy session when you've been feeling absolutely great but know you have to dredge up something to talk about in the truth chair. I'd reached my limits; I was all talked out.

As the runs accumulated and the woods and Deering's mellifluous chatter got to work, I realised that my relationship with running was changing. It was no longer purely a balm for psychological pain, though that was part of it. It definitely wasn't a stick I was using to beat myself, or the root of my identity as it had been when I was a teenager. As I got older and matured, it had become that most wonderful activity: a gift to give myself. Free and constantly accessible, that land of milk, sweat and honey on the other side of the front door. As I get older, I tend to judge the validity of an experience on how I feel directly after it and whether I want to repeat it. A heavy night's booze, for example, leaves me psychologically dismantled, unable to contemplate the simplest social transaction without dissolving into an anxious foetal ball in the corner. There is little desire to do it again. Similarly, after half an hour on social media rowing with a stranger about politics I throw the iPhone down in shaky disgust; I have been mugged by a bad habit. These are moments of weakness, activities I succumb to, that lack value. Running had become something different; I emerged from an hour in the woods cleansed, connected and regenerated. It had intrinsic value in itself.

Now, at the age of 47, I saw with blinding clarity that I wasn't running away from anything. It was more a running towards.

14

Early March. You are my hero

As March crested, signalling seven weeks before the big day, the running dial had switched up a notch. For the first time I was actually training properly for a marathon, following a schedule. Every week: one long run, two speed sessions, parkruns at the weekend. On the other days I'd be dipping into Highgate Woods for some good times. I was running six days a week, with total mileage regularly spiking above 40 miles. Interim races that I had put in to prepare for the marathon showed that the work was paying off.

The Watford half marathon returned a time of 01:27:18. A month later, the Bath half marathon was even better. 01:25:02. Both races felt profoundly different to anything I'd recently experienced. Mentally, I was stronger than before. In training I'd been regularly beating down my inner Snoop; pain had been welcomed, revelled in. During races it had become almost nourishing. I'd seek it out, feasting on it. It was a new feeling – on the verge of anger, but fun too, attractive in its way. It was like mining an inner bubble of furious joy. I'd connected running to my ego again; I was competing, but from a more centred place.

Short fast steps had become my motto. I'd been YouTubing Alberto Cova, an old hero of mine. Cova was an Italian long-distance runner of the mid '80s, an Olympic and World Champion over 5000 and 10,000 metres. As a teenager I'd connected with his daring sprint finishes, his modest demeanour, his light, quick steps. Thirty years later, I channelled Cova on the streets of Bath, albeit a more portly, middle-aged version. Regardless, I felt real progress.

After races, I'd relax in that gorgeous post-race glow, like the chill-out zone after raves but way healthier. I'd open up, babbling away to fellow runners freely without a care. I felt open to all, as if a film that separated me from the world had been removed; a truth had been established and settled on.

Bodily changes manifested themselves. The bathroom scales, like my belt buckles, spoke a wondrous message. Ridges on my legs appeared, which I hadn't felt before. There is an undeniable vanity to running fitness. For me, it's mostly in the legs: I love a sculptured set of oaky pins, they don't have to be mine. Just the sight gives me great pleasure. My mind was clearer; it sounds stupid, but the lightness in my body rippled through me. I felt almost reptilian, like my senses were more acute.

While at rest, I began to glimpse the deep attraction of running and what it gives us. I share these thoughts in the spirit of generosity – and give them in the knowledge that really, I know nothing.

(Strap yourselves in.)

In short, as well as fitness and all the obvious physical stuff – the endorphins, weight loss, lustrous hair, clear complexion and legs of a stallion – it strikes me that running offers up something very simple and also very seductive: a certain sense of control.

As life progresses, things get complicated. At home, as we get older we may very well gravitate naturally and gratefully to the bottom of the food chain. It's a nice view from back there and it's lovely to look after folk, to be the frame while your kids paint the picture and all that malarkey – but it's not stress-free, is it? Bills add up. Repairs need doing. The multiple minor things to keep on top of, the daily, weekly and monthly effort to keep the family ship sailing can leave the skipper a bit ragged and under celebrated. At work also, things get a bit muddy. You might get stalled in middle management; be adrift and alone at the top, or desperately clawing away near the bottom. You might be labouring in a field dominated by events you cannot control and judged by metrics that you barely understand and for which you have little respect. You could be at the whim of fashion, the shifting tides of identity politics. It's chaotic and that's just your stuff, we haven't even read the papers yet, or dipped our toe in the foetid excesses and tribal troll fest of social media. That daily bombardment of Twitter beefs, Facebook rants, Instagram fantasies of over-designed nonsense – all contriving to leave you both full to the brim and undeniably empty at the same time. It's very hard to get a handle on and keep abreast of – if I can say that as a cisgendered, heteronormative, white male drenched in privilege.

By contrast, running offers a personal and direct correlation between effort and reward that is deeply attractive. To be blunt, if you train hard, you *will* be rewarded. There are no short cuts, which at this stage in history makes it profoundly compelling. We are constantly searching for quick routes to success. New writers, for example, are coached to increase social media reach, gain followers, go viral – anything but work hard on actual writing. Everybody's getting better at marketing, but nobody's trying to get better at the thing in itself. The value of experience is being constantly eroded in the search for the newest, most sophisticated methodologies. Running doesn't say that. There's no third party or uncontrollable elements (weather excluding). It's simply you, your body and what you choose to do with it. Running says: *Everything you do, your body will remember and adapt to. Run 15 miles today, and in three days you will be stronger.*

If you run fast regularly, you will become a faster human. There's no intermediary; just yourself, your training and an immediate effect. Every run is an experience that you are giving yourself, which adds to the whole that you are personally creating. Every day a paragraph, every week a chapter. It's not going through head office, it's not being commissioned. It cannot be taken away from you. You earn this, you keep it. It contains within it a timeless, inescapable justice. There is no magic (except the breathtaking intricacy of human biology and its adaptive qualities), just hard yards. And the metrics are easily understood: time itself. Absolute, unarguable, pure time measured in hours, minutes and seconds. (In yer face, Matthew and your graded change!) A totally objective measure, with which you have an entirely subjective relationship. Running lies firmly in your control.

Nobody is going to grab you at Mile 16 and usher you off the course *because the company's restructuring.* You will not be told at Mile 20 that you're no longer needed because *we're relocating to Frankfurt.* It's your gig, your race, your terms. You can earn this. And by putting a race in the diary, you create an event in the near future over which you can exert a healthy element of control. You might not be able to stop your teenage daughter going out with an unsavoury boyfriend, but you can squeeze in 7 miles midweek. Your individual efforts at recycling may seem pathetic in the grander scheme of things but you can meet up with mates on a Sunday morning, run 18 miles and then have a hot bath with a cup of tea, job done.

You are the agent of your own transformation. To see the change in your body, in your speed and stamina and know that you and only you have caused it is empowering. Be the change!

An event just formalises the arrangement, codifies a contract you've drawn up yourself. This is on you and you alone.

It's your sacrifice that you freely choose. You train yourself.

You do this because the race demands it. The race is a metaphor. A dazzlingly simple metaphor for your relationship with the world.

It offers up a chance of an entirely self-created day's drama, where you can be the hero. And you compete on a level playing field on entirely your own terms. Not everyone can win the race, but everyone can meet their goal – or, if falling short, give it their very best. It offers up a safe arena of conflict, where the more you give, the more you get. It's effort, pain, determination – all the traditional undervalued stuff.

In a culture drowning in irony, where to be trying hard is viewed as an insult, running exists in a completely unironic space. It's the Tom Cruise of hobbies, not cool but mightily enjoyable.

As I began to get faster, tectonic plates shifted inside my psyche. I was going for this time, but more than that – and don't worry, I'm aware of how ridiculous this sounds – the marathon was giving me an opportunity to see my life in a more dramatic context. There was a sense that if I grabbed it, it would fulfil me in ways I could not even have imagined.

About six weeks away from the marathon, I crossed a Rubicon in my mind. Probably because I was seeing such results, I got carried away by a momentum that I had created for the first time in my adult life. Stepping off the bathroom scales one morning, having registered my lowest weight in years, I decided to give the marathon absolutely everything. Everything in every moment, both on the day and in the remaining build-up. All sense of any begrudging commitment had gone, I was all in. It felt very calming and simultaneously explosively exciting. I had chosen to cast aside my velour armour of domestic mediocrity and clothe myself in a grander costume.

(Cue the music; anything you fancy, something inspirational.)

From this moment forth, as I gazed into the bathroom mirror that needed a new light fitting (damn you, House!) I was no longer Paul Tonkinson, father, son, husband, Coffee Circus-dwelling procrastinator, supermarket stalker and Oddbins enthusiast.

I had gone down to the river, laid down my arms, and dunked my head fulsomely in the waters of total surrender. Refreshed, I had shaken my hair free and dried myself off with the towels of absolute freedom. Self-doubt was vanquished. The urge to self-sabotage, destroyed. I walked the Earth reborn, anew.

From this point I was now a Hero.

Another caveat: when I say *hero*, I don't mean an actual hero. It's obviously not have-a-go stuff. I'm not talking firemen, nurses, army, police officers. True heroism, I think, is revealed spontaneously. This is a heroism we can train for, a more manageable, planned, accessible heroism available to us all, if you fancy it.

Mile 16. Isle of Dogs. Peaking

Goal time – 01:48:15. Actual time – 01:47:56

Ten miles to go, and I am in a little window of pure energy and motion. I'm tired, yes, but not quite, to use the technical term, knackered. I am completely extended, but my form is fluid. It's like the giddy stage of drunk when you're chatting to everyone but just on the right side of it. There's no embarrassment yet. It's that moment when you're leaning forward on your stool, released from all notions of decorum, and for an all too brief second you glimpse the transitory nature of existence and decide to celebrate every second with anyone who happens to be in the vicinity, liberated as you are from any false notions of separateness from your fellow humans. This normally happens round about the time the shots kick in and just before you're strong-armed out by the bouncers. You're drinking those drinks that are on fire or which need to be chased down with salt and lemon. You're on top! Holding forth! The world's a massive chat show and you're the host. A cosmic Graham Norton, the centre of and creator of the storm. Nothing could happen to disturb the equilibrium, *you are* the equilibrium in this all too brief flicker before you descend into sentiment and repetition. For now, you are triumphant. You have expanded yourself as a context. You are open, fully stretched into the world and, as a result, absolutely invincible.

As I charge through the docks, I'm inevitably approaching the Wall. That's for certain, but I'm completely beyond concern. My limbs ache, but their function is not compromised. It's possible that I am running looser and with more freedom than I ever have or ever will again. I am beyond doubt surfing that perfect seam of effort and reward. Input/output systems in perfect harmony. Soon a miserable fatigue will attack my mind and body. I know that, but in this moment I feel truly fit, as fit as I have ever been. Wonderful. I've just run 16 miles faster than I have ever done in my life.

The crowd are buoyant. It's like they are singing to us. I feel very close at this point to my fellow runners, privileged to be part of this charging cavalry. We are not competing, we're bringing out the best in each other. Snippets of chat happen. *Looking good.* Or *Push, push.* Sometimes water is shared. Joseph would be pleased, we are enjoying ourselves.

There are 10 miles to go. A countdown of sorts. The pace is unrelenting, possibly even speeding up just a tad. In 10 minutes or so things will change, the gels can only do so much. The water, the sports drinks and other accoutrements of the modern-day marathon, which protect you from the ravages of the distance, will fall away and limitations will be encountered. Then the struggle will all be in the mind – but for now my legs pitter-patter softly, skimming down the street while my arms work in a seamless counterbalance. *Cova! Cova!* I am making hay while the sun shines, completely lost in the act of running. It's at times like this that I imagine I have found my perfect expression as a human being, beyond comedy, beyond family. Is this my name, my signature? This timeless surge into the next step? I'm on the Marine Drive again at 12 years old, stepping forth with a boundless energy into a limitless future. I am pure form. I am running like an animal. There is a recklessness to it, the slight increase in pace, like legging it towards a cliff edge.

It could be argued, I am enjoying myself too much.

Perhaps my mental reserves, which I will desperately need later, are being plundered to no great purpose. Or perhaps I am fuelling myself, perhaps it is this joy that will help propel me through what is to come. This moment that I have earned in training, of smooth physical ecstasy, will bed into my muscles and ease my passage as legs get heavier and darkness descends.

For now, at this very second, I am light, pure light, smiling fiendishly, tearing through the Isle of Dogs.

15

Six weeks to go. The life of the hero

Insights abounded at this stage of the training, accumulating on an almost daily basis.

On a very simple level, I wasn't thinking very much. That in itself is significant. Oh, how I love a good think, though it's really a contradiction in terms! Like a serve and volley tennis player, I'm at my best when there's no time to think and I'm at the net, acting on pure reflex. On top, dominant, fizzing backhands, forehands, slamming winners or teasing delicate drop volleys. Throw up a lob and I'm in bits, I'm falling over, missing the ball. Suddenly I'm not playing anymore, I'm in a psychodrama: it's all or nothing, the ball's in the air and I'm projecting all over it. It's thought that paralyses me. Again, maybe it's childhood stuff coming in through a different window. There was a lot of time alone, long hours when I was consigned to the garden as punishment, sometimes entire summer holidays. Being trapped at her behest created an exhausting tension, while awaiting her arrival and almost inevitable violence. To this day, I'm no good at waiting and can get unnecessarily tense before the most mundane of meetings.

The axis of my life has lurched firmly over to the running dial. If I'm not running, I'm exploring the possibilities of domestic workouts. I see exercise opportunities everywhere. On the bottom stair I'm teasing out a slightly sore calf muscle; on my son's pull-up bar I'm dangling for a second like a fruit bat, stretching out my lumbar. A waiting kettle never boils, I've realised, but it does provide a decent planking opportunity. Dynamic hoovering loosens up my core muscles. Stacking the dishwasher gives me a chance to perfect my squatting technique.

I am, in short, a right pain in the arse round the house.

At this stage my fitness is growing exponentially. I'm leaner and sharper – though the mind still needs work.

One night at training I'd chased a club mate around some long reps at the track – an exhausting session in freezing conditions. As we chatted afterwards, Sarah dispensed some encouraging words, saying I'd feel the quality on the day of the marathon. I shared how tough I found these nights, how difficult I found it to tolerate discomfort, to quell the inner voices begging to slow down. She just said matter-of-factly, 'Oh, you just don't think about it at all. You just do it.' She didn't present it like a Nike advert; this wasn't offered as an inspirational maxim, more as a statement of fact. Thinking does not make this easier, so think as little as possible. We are running, what's to think about? Lock in and go. Push, push. This is training, it's going to hurt, don't think about the pain, don't give it any more respect than it deserves, just accept it and move on. When you see top athletes on the box, look at their face. They do not seem lost in thought. Rather, they are there but not there; ethereal even. They only register distress, if any, in the last few strides. They cross over the finishing line, and it's then that, bizarrely, they often immediately collapse lifelessly to the ground like a set of pipe cleaners, while race organisers cluster around them for a nice photo. They are, to put it mildly, completely spent.

So what's happening?

I would wager that during the race they are experiencing incredible stress but are refusing to identify with it. Instead, they are ploughing through. There's a performative aspect to running, which is part of the fun. It's fun to wave, high-five, shout and banter with spectators. On the flip side, sometimes that can tip over into an exaggerated self-pity. I've done it myself: halfway through a bad patch in a marathon I've found myself changing my style slightly in front of the audience just to show that despite my slow pace I am really trying hard. It's like a parody of effort, trying to rinse the crowd of some more cheers, playing to the gallery. Once I turn the corner and there's nobody there, my style reverts to a more economical cadence.

The further up the field you get, the less showy the runners seem to be. It was noticeable that Group A on a Tuesday ran in a more tidy fashion than anyone else with less obvious fatigue, but after the session they were exhausted on the floor, occasionally vomiting.

One night I saw a young athlete suddenly veer off the track during a set of fast sprints and sit down abruptly. He's an extremely quick young man with a softly spoken demeanour. I sidled alongside him to make sure he was OK, offering up my lack of any medical knowledge.

'I'm fine,' he said. 'It's just that if I push it too hard, I can't see anymore. I go blind for a bit. So I sit down. It passes very quickly.'

Blind?

This obviously is madness, and brings up all kinds of questions. Specifically, should we be introducing guide dogs at training?

But he did show me how focused the faster runners are on pushing through barriers. I've got no interest in trashing myself this hard; in truth, my lack of talent doesn't warrant it. I'm operating on way more mellow parameters, but I could see there was something I could learn from this. More and more I began to see my fellow club mates less as runners and more as pain gurus, experts in oxygen deprivation. So I borrowed from them as much as I could, despite being much slower. With mental energy at a premium, it's more tiring to fight pain, so I tried to combine physical relaxation at speed with mental fortitude, a Zen-like disassociation from and acceptance of pain. As a result, training got easier.

Off the track, life too was simpler.

The torrent of thoughts racing through my mind had been miraculously stilled. On both a conscious and subconscious level I had completely surrendered to the event. This meant that for a brief period of time I existed on a level beyond temptation. Like a stick of rock, I read 'commitment' all the way through, the event being my only frame of reference. It's only at moments like this you see clearly how much temptation is laden into everyday life; we live in a society built for solace, surrounded by substances designed to soothe, not nourish. That spring, the Marathon led me through the decision-making process, becoming my go-to reference point. What a relief! I had a framework that allowed me to opt for the right choices.

In the supermarket: *Shall I have cheap sugary biscuits or more expensive proteinaceous nuts? Ask the Marathon.*

Driving past Oddbins: *Do I nip in for a cheeky bottle or content myself with water? Ask the Marathon.*

On a weekend: *Do I go to the party on Saturday night or get an early night for tomorrow's run? Ask the Marathon.*

The Marathon held me in its arms, the Marathon wanted the best for me. To drink, to overindulge was to disrespect the opportunity it was giving me to live and compete intensely. It had fed me into a value system that was utterly real. All thoughts of magic had gone, I was earning the day in every moment.

I was breathing the rarified air of the zealot. It felt brilliant, and I realised how hard it actually is to live a life of moderation. Really we are designed to live and crave the extreme. Moderation is insanely difficult, carrying as it does within it the seeds of self-destruction.

Consider the absurdity of the 'just one drink' pledge when out. You're dealing with a substance that is extremely nice and by nature intoxicating, blurring as it does the boundaries between rational and irrational thought. You know that one of the pleasures of it is that it leads you into making decisions that you wouldn't normally make. In fact, that's why you drink in the first place, to release you from the tyranny of logic and right decisions. So, instead of foregoing the substance in question to give yourself half a chance of a decent evening and, more importantly, a productive next day, you decide to have just a little bit of it. Knowing full well that the reason you're having a little bit of it is to make you boozy enough to have a lot more. Next thing you know, you're in a cab to a jazz club in Dalston with all your old mates, like a day trip for the cast of *Cocoon*.

Moderation is the enemy. Moderation opens the door to food, booze and hedonism and expects us to have the wherewithal to shut it again. An edge of fanaticism keeps things simpler.

No booze, no biscuits. Water, nuts and fruit from now on. *The Marathon. Ask the Marathon.* Every day I was writing the script for my future; it felt focused and fun. After years of wallowing in reasonableness and a hellish compromise, I had gone all in with my inner extremist and I lived in a world beyond questions. The strange and wonderful thing was, it didn't feel extreme. It felt utterly peaceful and laughably easy. As Chris Eubank once said: the hardest thing is the easiest thing: sacrifice. And it was totally natural, organic. I was reminded of that saying – I'm nicking it, I read it somewhere recently – along the lines of *You don't think your way into a new way of living; you live yourself into a new way of thinking.* This change in me wasn't imposed through will, it was nurtured and emerging from within. Why would I want to hex something that was so right?

The truth is, when you're running all the time, you don't want to have a drink because you see it as poisoning the well. There's a purity to the process. Likewise, you don't want to wake up full of half a packet of choc 'n' nut cookies. It will slow you down.

This didn't mean the life of a hero was easy. Some days it was tough; the training had ramped to hitherto unreached levels: 50-mile weeks, even 55. I was constantly tired, but extremist tricks were coming out to amp up the effect of training. I had read lots of running books, chatted about running on the podcast, and over the years I had accumulated a pool of knowledge. Marginal gains became my new buzzword; any little advantage I'd plunder to get faster. Weight loss became increasingly important. Keeping the Mayr pounds off was not easy, tricks were required. Multiple tracksuits when running helped, as did long runs on an empty stomach. Twenty miles before a very late breakfast trained my body to utilise fuel better, even though I think it probably comes under the category of inadvisably hard training.

I had gone beyond normal. Every day was a constant dare to go further, get stronger.

You'll be pleased to know that even with this fanaticism there were boundaries I couldn't cross, sacrifices that I couldn't justify however much sense they made. In terms of diet, there were many changes I made, and many more I could make – but there was one I couldn't continue with or justify on any level. It was an experience that plunged me into a temporary but total abyss, an existential crisis that made me question the very purpose of life itself.

It was the day I ate a gluten-free Jaffa Cake.

Now I have to confess I am a Jaffa Cake fan. I can pop a packet easily. To me it offers the perfect combination of wafery cake, chocolate and just a hint of fruit, which, however sugary, provides at least the illusion of health. Still, hard to pretend it's anything but sheer gluttony as the last Jaffa sidles down your gullet, leaving you looking at that suddenly no longer magic blue box with the orange zesty design. Was this me living, as the kids say, my best life? What could I do with the marathon coming up?

To exist without any Jaffa Cakes seemed unthinkable. To continue the periodic gorge fest was lunacy. I did the rational thing, I compromised: I went gluten-free. I figured this would not be too much of a stretch, I might need to go gluten-free anyway. (It's often been suggested to me that I might be a bit overgassy. But it's never been diagnosed and to make a medical condition out of something in which I take great pleasure seems a tad churlish.)

So I went to Tesco and took the gluten-free bungee jump. They still looked like Jaffa Cakes, if slightly smaller. Surely they couldn't be that different. I launched in. My first impression was the total lack of sugar. The chocolate didn't taste of chocolate. Rather, it was a thin illusory border of a substance that sort of looked like chocolate but did something totally different to the tongue, coating it in a slightly sticky, annoying tang. Similarly, to experience the layer of orangey sweet fruit was to be subjected to a deceitful, flavourless goo.

What was happening? The culprit was the cake, the substance that holds the whole enterprise together. In the original, this is the Jaffa, the upbeat, soft, optimistic cake that cradles the chocolate, providing a platform for the orangey fruit wondrousness. It's the very foundation of the Jaffa Cake experience. This mutant, gluten-free concoction inflicted a dry inhuman texture to the throat, a sawdusty strangulation that even a cup of tea couldn't salvage. It was, without doubt, the worse thing I've ever tasted – and I once baked my own bread in school home economics, took it home and ate it.

My argument/problem with this monstrosity is twofold. Primarily, of course, it's a taste issue. Even my gluten-free friends, upon hearing of my encounter with a gluten-free Jaffa Cake, agreed that sometimes the gluten-free versions just don't cut it. They were, they admitted, a poor substitute.

On a more philosophical note, I ask simply, why? Why not just accept that the essence of the Jaffa Cake is inextricably bound with gluten? What is there in the original Jaffa Cake that makes you so keen that you can't let go? Having sampled the alternatives, I would argue that one of the key elements is gluten!

To be fair, my extreme response to the gluten-free Jaffa was probably exacerbated by my extreme fatigue at the time. Very simply, I was tired all the time. I'd fall asleep in public libraries, or have to sit down suddenly and rehydrate in shopping malls. Supermarkets were tougher now; lost in a witless fatigue, I'd end up mouth agape in the wrong aisle, adrift in wild cheese and wine fantasies. Ra would rescue me, take me by the hand and usher me away to the safety of the fresh fruit section. At parties, I'd find myself feeling awkward on the fringes. I'd cracked the drinking thing, I wasn't even thinking about it by this stage. The machine didn't need it, but this left me a bit alienated. Concerned friends would notice my distant demeanour and the slightly sunken cheekbones and enquire about my health. I'd mutter about training, mileage, reducing injury risk. They'd feign interest for a while, but the chasm between us was too wide, I was on a mission. We'd arrange to meet post-marathon when I'd be myself again, then they'd touch my arm with a quizzical expression and mosey off.

The truth is, I had never felt more alive, more utterly myself. Every moment had purpose, every action fed a larger intention.

The Marathon!

16

Five weeks before the marathon. Cuba

As a hero you will be beset on all sides by obstacles and by inducements to drink that threaten the sanctity of the training process. These must be grappled with ruthlessly (*Marathon says no*). I found friends' parties fairly easy to knock back; my wife's the main attraction anyway. Sunday lunches can be smothered with sparkling mineral water; a subtle exit to the living room at an opportune moment to watch football can leave you sober by the end of the afternoon.

Family holidays are a way tougher proposition. It's embedded in the very structure of holidays. They are a break. A chance to relax, live differently, let loose. If you can't chill then, with the family, what's the point?

Cuba had been in the diary for half a year. Five weeks before the event, appalling timing for the hero.

I had a private moment with the Marathon prior to departure, ushered him into the bedroom for a tête-á-tête.

I said, 'It's not serious, why are you frowning? We can do this and emerge stronger.'

The Marathon looked at me sternly. 'I think you should cancel the holiday.'

I said, 'I can't. It's non-refundable.'

The Marathon, although existing on a quantum plane beyond money, relented. 'Fair enough, money's tight, you can train while you're there. But go easy, I know what you're like.'

To which I replied, 'You're going to have to trust me.'

This was good, I had an angle. I was not going on holiday, it was a training week in Cuba. If anything, freed from the daily travails of driving to gigs, late nights and family responsibilities I should get more training done.

As the holiday progressed, however, the situation got more complicated.

Not only, I realised, was it billed as a holiday, it also contained within it the two words that strike terror in the heart of any heroes, particularly marathon runners, five weeks – a mere 35 days – before the big day: All Inclusive.

From the moment we entered the marble and expansive lobby of this very reasonably priced Cuban pleasure palace, it was all laid on for us. Food. Booze. Cakes. Everything. The devil was everywhere, calling me. I broke into a cold sweat as we approached check-in. This all-inclusive business was news to me.

Over the years our family has evolved into quite a traditional structure. Family members assume roles, positions are allocated. For instance, my wife has secured sole control over booking the holidays. This is just one of the tasks that falls into her department. Other things in her department include kids' clothes; school liaison, friends liaison, relatives liaison (involving birthday admin, also remembering all friends' birthdays, names of their kids, remembering dates of births of *our* kids); household furnishings, interior design; the general mystery of household clothes washing and distribution; all forms of insurance; ringing handymen when I can't do anything (and I can't do anything); pet safety; storage; the garden; 70% of food preparation and general ideas as to where everything is.

My department involves most of the food buying (I get to chat to folk in the village); all forms of waste disposal, including human and pet waste; the dispensing of cash; kid transport; dead mouse extraction; the opening of jars; all levels of the house beyond a certain height; scaring the kids; loading the car; and, of course, security – the locking of doors, checking of windows, dealing with people who call at the house, scouting the perimeter of public events, socially profiling the people who are present and mentally rehearsing exit strategies in the event of attack. It's a 24-hour risk assessment gig combined with a hefty dose of catastrophising. This can be very tiring and from a distance might look as if I'm doing nothing at all

Try not to judge. It's a system that works.

But as I said, all aspects of the holiday are NMD (not my department). Everything – location, length of stay, method of travel, passports, insurance. She loves it, always googling away at the kitchen table. I take no interest at all, except choice of the hire car and a brief glimpse at the price (ouch!). I see it as a form of lucky dip. Setting off with only the barest idea where we are going.

I do, however, retain the right to complain on arrival.

'How has this happened? What have you done?' I hissed in her ear as the hotel porters circled like sharks for our bags.

'What do you mean?'

'The All fucking Inc.' I can be a tad moody when blindsided. I was also hot and bothered, and ridiculously overdressed. Velour and Cuba were proving to be a terrible combination.

'I thought it'd be nice to relax from all this marathon training,' she replied. 'You've been a bit distant.'

'Distant? I've been focused. I've broken through. After years of self-sabotage, I've achieved nirvana. I have a goal and a purpose. I am a happy warrior. A hero.'

She looked at me disdainfully for a second, peering over her sunglasses as if perusing an antique that didn't particularly interest her. 'If we check in quick, we can have a mojito before dinner. It's Mexican night.'

I sat down to get my bearings. The kids, having effortlessly adapted to the new all-inclusive reality, plundered the hotel Wi-Fi while ordering fatty lattes.

Feeling a sensation of light panic, I scanned the perimeter. Chunky Americans traversed the lobby, limping back to their rooms, sun-shocked after an afternoon at the pool. The sound of Bon Jovi rang through from the poolside bar, carried by laughter, splashes and the aroma of burgers.

My surroundings were seducing me. They were telling me I was on holiday with my family. I knew this was a falsehood; I was on a training camp with the Marathon.

At the other end of the lobby an extremely red-faced, shaven bald man of about 50 sat with his head back on a leather chair. Was he sleeping? It was hard to say. Even from a distance, where I was sitting, I could see the moisture mottling his forehead, running down his neck onto his matted hairy chest, tufts of which peeked out at the top of a plain light blue T-shirt. Sweat marks were proceeding in a semicircular formation from his armpits. He'd obviously overdone it in the midday heat. Feminists would say that his sitting stance was manspreading. To me it looked like a posture of deep supplication as he surrendered to whatever fate had in store for him; any sense of decorum was fading fast as he unfastened the top button on his grey canvas shorts.

Staff hovered nervously, urgently shouting into mobiles. A mousy-haired young boy of about seven years old, wearing a Minnesota Vikings T-shirt, viewed him from 10 metres away, absent-mindedly stuffing what looked like a caramel cream donut into his gaping mouth.

Historically, I'm not that good in an all-inclusive environment; our only previous encounter had been at a Club Med in Sicily. This was in my not-really-running-much days. It took us a few days to get our heads round the simple concept. We were quick enough to get the knack of the food aspect of the all-inclusive holiday, settling in to the sustained assault. Three courses minimum, and double desserts. The Italian cuisine was as uncompromisingly excellent as you'd expect: a vast array of pastas and salads, fresh fish, meats, and an obscenely elaborate smorgasbord of cheese, all chased down with sumptuous gelato, tiramisus, brûlées. Heaven for family Tonks.

Free drink, though, was a worry. At the first lunch we clocked but refused the wines on offer. Our fellow holidaymakers launched in with abandon. At breakfast we witnessed rambunctious, red-faced Russians cheerfully plonking small bottles of vodka into their espressos, lustily singing songs and shouting at bar staff. Bathers poolside seemed to be snoozing a bit too deeply and waking up too dishevelled for it to be mere fatigue. It was fairly obvious a lot of quaffing was going on. A holiday was happening within the holiday and we hadn't quite hopped aboard. For a couple of days we resisted the inevitable, existing like Puritans off a sole bottle with our meal of an evening. The children were our priority. After all, we'd chosen the holiday for the sports facilities; the play provision, family time.

Two days in, we wilted at a beach bar as we gazed out to sea, losing ourselves in the deep blue hues of the Mediterranean sparkling and bouncing in the midday heat. As we watched bathers frolicking in the ocean, a light breeze caressed our temples, banishing our misgivings. Resolve seemed suddenly futile. What were we doing? We were on holiday surrounded by unlimited booze. Let's get on the guzzle!

This signalled the part of my life that I like to call the Gérard Depardieu phase.

We ordered a *light* bottle, polished it off before the starters had finished, then ordered another. A pattern quickly asserted itself.

Drunk at dinner. Kip in the apartment. Drunk in the evening. At least two bottles each a day with dessert wine to follow. The kids can find their way to the pool, everyone's happy.

As a test of our willpower, it was an undeniable failure. As an experiment in alcoholism, it was a resounding success, a glorious descent into anarchy.

Over the week I found that I enjoyed the fuzzy-headed resignation as basic words and logic began to elude me. It was a befuddlement that was most agreeable; after all, it would last only a minute or two. If I felt befuddled, it was because I was conscious; if I was conscious, I was on my way to more wine.

Weight gain was a bit jarring, but from a certain angle I began to look a bit more authoritative. The kids loved it as the wallet was loosened: it was an orgy of ice cream cones drizzled with parental guilt.

THIS COULD NOT HAPPEN IN CUBA. I WOULD NOT JEOPARDISE THE EVENT AT THIS VERY IMPORTANT TIME IN THE TRAINING CYCLE.

Standing up in a rather distracted fashion, I wandered over to the other side of the lobby. The bar was rammed as busy bartenders danced and shimmied in a vain attempt to satisfy a frenzied mob of mostly middle-aged cocktail fans. They'd paid for all inclusive – and they were going to get it. Hard-working, hard-partying Americans with rock ballads in their heart and everything paid for; it was a kind of paradise. I've always loved holidaying with Americans. I have a deep and unrestrained love for the country, I'm a sucker for it. When I was a teenager, my wall was dominated by a huge poster of Bruce Springsteen. At university, my dissertation was on Woody Allen. My favourite stand-up of all time, the reason I did stand-up comedy, was Richard Pryor. You're already privy to my Snoop Dogg obsession. My kids have middle names (Cassius, Marcellus) in honour of Muhammad

Ali (born Cassius Marcellus Clay). I'm a *Sopranos*-loving, Saul Bellow-reading, Madonna vogueing, coffee to go with blueberry muffin freak. The Stars and Stripes anthem stirs my heart with an unexplainable passion. *God save every man!* I love the optimistic swirling nature of this great experiment over the Atlantic from us, its wild excesses and manic energy. New York thrills me to the core. Santa Monica beach is possibly my favourite spot on Earth.

Even so, this was bad for me, this could be really bad. The voice of the Marathon began to sound more distant; maybe it was at the bar with everyone else, ordering a cocktail.

As my wife sorted the rooms, I gravitated closer to our struggling, sweating friend in the pale blue T-shirt. On holiday I'm a drifter. I tend to disengage even further (if that's possible) from the everyday mechanics of efficiency and organisation to partake in bizarre interactions with fellow travellers. His condition had noticeably worsened in the last five minutes, his head now lolled backwards more acutely, a faint white froth played at the edges of his lips. As I got closer, I saw stains on his T-shirt, the smudge of some kind of cake, a deep red hue that, I later discovered, was a sour cherry gin sling.

'Is he OK?' I asked the uniformed staff, who didn't seem as concerned as previously.

'Are you a doctor?' they asked matter-of-factly.

'No,' I replied. 'Problem?'

'Yes. We have called a doctor. They should be here soon.'

'Sunburn?'

The response came in such nonchalant fashion that it felt like they were relating a common occurrence. 'Mr Massey is having a heart attack.'

What had we signed up for? This Cuban cocktail cardiac hell?

(You'll be pleased to know that Mr Massey made a full recovery. I met him on the beach four days later as we both took shelter from the sun. He was a chastened, gentle man from Ohio who worked in educational administration and seemed determined from that day forth to extend his life indefinitely through the endless sipping of Coke Zeros.)

Ra had done her homework, the rooms were lovely.

The kids had their own three-bed mosh pit while the aged holiday lovebirds were sequestered in a small but perfectly functional den for the week. I looked forward to settling in to my usual pattern *en vacances*: ignoring my family's desire for trips, staying in the air-conditioned rooms to avoid the scorching heat and trying to restrict spending. To me, as a Northerner, and a Yorkshireman to boot, one of the joys of an all inclusive is that you've paid for everything, there's no need to spend any more cash. In fact, much fun can be had totting up how little you've spent on a daily basis, every potentially spontaneous moment of fun becoming an instructional opportunity to educate the kids on the theory of budgeting. I was elated to discover the Marathon is also a skinflint (although occasionally insisting on overpriced energy balls or protein shakes). Families aren't. Families see the all inclusive as a springboard into further spending on items not covered by the all-inclusive umbrella. Outvoted and overpowered by notions of holiday fun, I acquiesced – and the vulgar spending splurge began.

Ice creams by the beach. (Is this really necessary? Sold!) Ice-cold Cokes, also by the beach. (When we've bottled water in the room? Sold.)

Locals hawked dubious ocean-bound experiences to my family, and I yielded, without experiencing them myself. On a good day I'd reach the beach for an hour or so and watch the kids snorkel and kayak their way through what little money we had remaining. It was gorgeous, but way too hot for me. I walked around with a white towel on my head, waiting for evening, when it was cool enough to go for a run.

Hotel Melia Marina was on the Varadero peninsula, which stretched 5 to 6 miles or so back to civilisation along a very straight, pancake-flat coastal road, with very hard but smooth pavements. It didn't take much imagination to figure that I could run out and back for a distance of about 10 miles. So that's what I did.

Six p.m. became my day's highlight. After a light lunch and an afternoon kip, I'd be stretching in the lobby, waiting for the baking heat to fall away from the day, so I could jog off into it.

It was beautiful skies and close nights for a week – and I loved it. It was also, after a day spent dodging requests from kids for goodies, gloriously free.

Running gives you a deeper experience of any holiday, it's an unfiltered sample of local life. On the way out I'd run past other resort hotels, yacht clubs, marinas, buses full of returning tourists after day trips out (extravagant fools freewheeling way beyond the dominion of the all inclusive).

After a few miles the paraphernalia of the tourism industry gave way to the harsh realities of the machine that supported it. Factories and power plants, massive waste disposal units. The air here was a tad more toxic, the road suddenly lined with boiler-suit-clad, ashen-faced, exhausted factory workers waiting for minivans to take them home. I must have been an exotic sight in my shorts and white T-shirt. Nobody else appeared to be running, and if they were, they certainly weren't running as far out of the resorts as I did.

Cuba is a poor country. It seems to be fashionable among the chattering classes in the UK to suggest that *now's the best time to go before it changes, and the Americans come,* but most locals I spoke to couldn't wait for it to change and for the Americans to come. Basic infrastructure is crumbling, buildings and roads in Havana are in a shocking state, old cars might look cool to us but are obviously a nightmare to run. The country, although beautiful and full of vibrant and resilient people, is in a state of absolute neglect.

Beggars are commonplace; I tried to keep change to hand, for tips and to shell out as much as possible, but on the second day I was shocked when a worker asked me as I ran by if I would give him my trainers. I said I would, but I needed them for the week. If he came to the hotel on the last day, I promised, he could have them. This seemed a compromise between me, the Marathon and a very sweet man, who I later discovered went by the name of Eric. He told me he wouldn't be allowed to enter the hotel, so we made a vague arrangement to meet outside on my last day.

I got to know that long, flat stretch of road very well over the week. The run became my highlight. And the week ended up being a 50-mile week, the highest so far. The road was so smooth that I would often push the pace on the way back. By this time, night would have fallen and I'd be on the road, dancing on and off the grass verge as cars approached. It had a reckless drama to it, flirting with high-speed collisions on a nightly basis.

The trick in a fast marathon is to run fast when you're really tired. Your style needs to be tight, and this is found through training. The body is a remarkable organism; it wants to conserve energy at all times. If you regularly run fast, it will find over time the most efficient way for you to do so. It won't look like everyone else. It will be your form and yours alone. Over that week in Cuba I bedded in my fitness, forcing my body to keep a steady fast pace, training my legs to keep turning over fast when they really didn't want to.

I felt very strong there; the Marathon was happy and family were very forgiving.

At about 7.30 p.m., I'd wash up in the lobby, spitting flies and drenched in sweat, a stark contrast to the linen-suited and booted early-evening dinner crowd. I'd walk on jelly legs, panting lustily back to the lovely cool air-conditioned room, and then go to the buffet for as much fresh fish as I could reasonably eat and, it has to be said, the odd dessert (I was on holiday).

In terms of the booze, the very occasional cocktail passed my lips (I'm no Calvinist), but overall, inebriation was avoided and purged every evening by the 10 miles. In truth I was saved by the failures of communism. The cocktails were fairly watered down, the food wasn't great. A familiar refrain at the buffet would come from an American tourist, they'd ask, 'Are you enjoying yourself?'

'YES I AM.'

'Will I return?' they'd rhetorically ask...

'Probably not!'

Supplies were limited, even though we were at the peak of Cuba's culinary potential. You could eat simply and healthily, but it wasn't the gorge fest that a lot of the Yanks wanted. On the whole, it's tough being on holiday when the local populace is so poor. My nightly runs gave me an insight into just how tough life was for workers. These people were tired out, underpaid, working in tough conditions. They were covered in soot, grubby and utterly exhausted. There I was, dancing past on a 10-miler. I was reminded, yet again, of how utterly fortunate, indulgent even, the whole enterprise is.

I'd been wondering if Eric would remember our rendezvous, and on the last night I left the hotel with a large bag for him, walking out into relative darkness. I quickly spotted him, smiling underneath the street lights in his all-orange work clothes. I gave him some running shoes, casual clothes and, much to his delight and on a whim, my running watch.

My kids came out to meet him. We exchanged best wishes for the future and shook hands warmly.

The next day, home.

17

The hardest week.
26 March – 2 April.
58½ miles

Mileage is the Holy Grail for marathon runners.

On a very simple level, the more you run, the faster you get. That's what training is, after all; a process of adaptation. I've seen runners massively improve by going from 30 miles a week to 40, and then the jump to 50 is quicker still. The jump from 50 to 60 marks more progress. This continues till the athlete is running more than 100 miles a week and his/her body spontaneously explodes halfway through a vigorous fartlek session. As the marathon got closer, I was racking up more miles than I'd ever done before. This is where it's extremely advantageous to be a stand-up comedian; you can have long baths in the afternoon, followed by a luxurious kip. The only problem is you might then have to do an eight-hour round trip to entertain 200 people in a bar in Nottingham who don't like you.

This week, at three weeks before the marathon, was my highest weekly mileage. It was the toughest week in terms of training that I had ever attempted.

Monday. Highgate Wood. 7½ miles
The classic loop.

I've run it so many times I could probably run it in my sleep, and during this period it's likely that I did. Here, I was coming off the back of a 52-mile week, very much into uncharted territory. Luckily I had a route that would husband me round it with a tender touch.

Situationally, I'm well set training wise. Within a minute of my front door I can be on the Parkland Way. This is an old disused rail track that joins Highgate Wood to the east with Finsbury Park to the west. I'm going in the direction of Highgate, mostly because I love woodland and the path is softer underfoot. It's a runner's paradise, a lovely tree-lined avenue. I feel sheltered from the relative harshness of the capital, nestling within nature's sweet bosom, passing through a very mellow crowd of dog walkers, nature lovers and fellow runners. After 10 minutes I briefly surface onto Archway Road, a reminder that I am, in fact, in London, before I zigzag on empty streets for a while. Then I plunge into the verdant dense foliage of Queen's Wood. A feeder wood for the more populated Highgate Wood. Now, I don't know my woodland; I love nature, but like to inhale its scent without knowing too much detail of the source. A brief google tells me that the woods contain 'English oak and occasional beech standing above hornbeam, midland hawthorn, hazel, mountain ash, field maple, cherry, holly and both species of lowland birch'. You get the drift; it is a woody abundance, a forest adventure. The ground flora, I've been told, is also extremely rich for somewhere so close to central London, including a large population of wood anemone, native bluebells, wood goldilocks and a thriving population of wood sorrel. You heard it here first. It's a treat to pad through; I love a soft surface underfoot, over time it's the pounding of the pavements that will injure you. To the sound of birdsong and the fluttering of squirrels, I can lose myself here quite happily in a profound reverie. I'm in that timeless zone again. I'm just moving, in the moment completely. I see it as time nicked from the normal hours and minutes system, time that will be added on at the end of life, like the football. So that's Queen's Wood, heartily recommended in North London; it's also got a great café on the corner near the road.

After the delight of Queen's Wood, it's a quick nip across Muswell Hill Road and you're in the jewel of this particular area's crown, Highgate Wood. Slightly less dense than Queen's, but long, swirling, soft pathways through the trees and a lovely grassy pitch in the middle. In summer this will be teeming with cricketers, yoga enthusiasts, dog walkers, Frisbee fanatics, people from all nations picnicking and enjoying the glories of an English summer. In winter it has a silent grandeur that can be breathtaking. Occasionally the kid in me takes over, I'll whip my trainers off and sprint full throttle across the grass barefooted. It's great for the legs to really fly on a soft surface, and it's good for the feet to feel the surface like that. This week saw none of that; I was wrapped up, moving steadily, my legs heavy but solid. In the middle of training like this, it's not all unfettered joy; some days it's just hard. You're building a jigsaw; every piece is important and sometimes you have to jam them in.

Once I've run round the woods a couple of times, I just reverse the route, back through Queen's, a little zigzag, and then let the last mile or so of the Parkland Way carry me homewards with its subtle downhill gradient.

That's Monday then. Less a run, more of a chat with an old friend.

Tuesday. Finsbury Park. 40-minute tempo run

This looks like nothing. In fact, these are the hardest sessions – and like all hard sessions they are incredibly useful. You basically run at just below race pace, which is awfully difficult when you're not in a race. Some runners do these on a weekly basis; they are the fast ones who exist on a plane of commitment that I manage only sporadically. I need company to do this. In fact, I need company to do any quality training, so it was back to the club for a jaunt round Finsbury Park. Only the London marathoners are up for mayhem such as this. Gavin is there, and Dominic too, stretching in the cool air that carries with it a suggestion of spring. The marathon is fast approaching. Dominic is posting some very fast times at races round the club circuit; Gavin is carrying an injury, which he accepts with good grace.

The bulk of the pack leaves us immediately behind. Dominic tags off the back of it, leaving me with the tangibly limping Gavin. There we stay for 40 minutes in a holding pattern, battling away as darkness falls, our breath pluming out in front of us as we mount our charge. Cor blimey, this is tough stuff. I did a lot of this as a youth, but the last five minutes or so really test my *don't think about it* mentality. The pain is relentless, searing into my legs, pinching my chest and weakening my arms, which are fairly useless at the best of times. Gavin is nibbling away behind me, but I manage to hold him off. Dominic has progressively pranced further and further away from me into the distance; he is a very natural runner, seemingly taking one stride to my three. For him, sub-3 seems assured. I'm in the frame, certainly, and have taken to telling everyone I'm going for it. This is a conscious move on my part. I've borrowed Gavin's tips on positive self-talk and have awakened the Giant Within. 'I am going for sub-3 in London,' I say. 'I'm going to do it.' Gavin loves it. 'That's it! That's what you have to say! Let's do it together,' he exhorts, grinning manically.

How can he even be contemplating sub-3? I wonder as I make my way to the car. His calf is, by all accounts, not fit for purpose, but it doesn't seem to bother him at all. He has a very mechanistic relationship with his body: he will fix it, or it will fix itself in motion. At the moment he can run, that's all. Normal notions of limitations and pain were left behind many years ago.

Wednesday. 6½ miles steady. Recording the podcast

By necessity this is a very easy run, conducted on grass, at conversational pace. It has to be, it's being recorded. Just Rob and I helping each other as the big day approaches. Listening to this podcast is to start off being privy to quite intense reflections on injury problems and managing high mileage. By the end, it's just two blokes screaming: 'Oi oi saveloy!' before descending into high-pitched giggling.

Thursday. My Initiation into the Ways of Yasso

Yasso is a key feature of any serious marathon preparation. It's a slightly strange session designed and popularised by running guru Bart Yasso, a kindly, inspirational American who's run more miles than you've had hot dinners, including marathons in all seven continents and the Badwater Ultramarathon, a 146-mile festival of suffering that takes you directly through Death Valley. (There, the highest recorded temperature is 56°C/134°F, and it's so hot that runners run on the white lines on the road; if they run on the tarmac, it melts their trainers.) Through a process of trial and error, good old Bart stumbled on what has become a popular method for predicting your marathon race time.

Race time prediction is an obsession for many runners. I get it, it's an attempt to reach into the future and shape it – similar, I suppose, to finding out what sex your baby's going to be before childbirth. Some like to know. I like to prepare as much as possible, sort the spare room, buy the baby basket and let the mysteries of the day unfold.

One method to predict times, which experience has proven to be fairly accurate, is to take the time for your half marathon, times it by two and then add 10 minutes. For the umpteenth time, every runner's different. Some are nippier over a short stretch and fade in the second half. Some are slow and steady merchants who fade less.

Yasso's method quickly gained currency, I believe because it's experiential. It's something you can do with other runners as part of the training programme. All you have to do is go down to the track and do 10 repetitions of 800 metres (jogging a recovery lap of two minutes between reps). Then divide your time for the reps by 10. That time in minutes and seconds should roughly equate to your marathon result in hours and minutes. So, for me, that means completing every rep in just under three minutes. Doable, but not very easy.

The Yasso session has achieved almost mythical status in club circles, so I feel quite excited as I warm up, preparing to pop my Yasso cherry. This time, no Dominic; he's probably in the stables somewhere or doing a dressage event. Plenty of others, though: Hoggy, Gavin, the usual suspects mustering around the start line and jogging on the spot, grinning nervously or yawning with a slight anxiety before coming to a silence. Then someone mutters 'The sooner we start, the sooner it will be over'; there is a collective pinging of Garmins and we're off, round the cold, dark track.

Within 80 metres, the athletic hierarchy has been established. Gavin's up for it and bolts away near the front, to remain there for the rest of the session. (How has he got so much faster in two days? I demand a drugs test.) This leaves me mopping up the back with Hoggy. It takes me a while to get to grips with the pace. On the very first rep I'm with Hoggy, but then he runs the recovery faster than me, spinning away with his low arms like a Christmas shopper running for a taxi. This leaves me with a gap of 10 metres or so, which persists into the next few reps. The good news is that each rep I run is bang on or just underneath three minutes; the bad news is, I'm dead last. Not a great fillip for the old confidence, but I beaver away on my own, trying to maintain some semblance of contact. As the reps go their merry way, I'm roundly lapped by most of the field but manage to catch Hoggy with three reps to go. We help each other to the end, taking the lead alternately to drag us through. Indeed, I find a bit of pace to pull away towards the end of the last one. Maybe it's the miles in Cuba, maybe it's an injection of momentum, but I'm finding strength in my legs that had hitherto not existed. Mentally, I am definitely getting tougher.

The average of my reps is 00:02:59.2. A portent perhaps? Am I on my way?

Now, many people pooh-pooh the accuracy of marathon predictions based on Yasso times. Needless to say, with these results I'm a convert.

Friday (rest)

When you're training very hard, recovery becomes an essential part of the programme. The muscles need to build up again, repair and strengthen. A rest day at this time is perfect.

Not that it's all easy. Turns out this is the day of the gluten-free Jaffa Cake experiment.

Saturday. 5-mile road race. Hoodwinking the Central Governor in Victoria Park

Quality training sessions are piling atop each other like a cardio club sandwich. A race, however, might be tricky. I'm still feeling traces of the Yasso in my legs as I warm up around the smooth flatlands of London's Victoria Park, perfect for running, a personal best arena of legendary status. The 5-miler is a rarely run distance. Loads of Heathsiders are in attendance, some preparing for the marathon and some just fancying a Saturday morning tear up.

This race is to give me a real boost. Mentally, it feels like I am exploring new territory.

I'd been introduced to and become fascinated by the concept of the Central Governor. To break it down, the Central Governor is said to be a self-monitoring reflex in the brain, which will not let you run so hard that you cause real damage to yourself. It's self-protective, an inbuilt brake mechanism that is constantly assessing the distance you have left to run, the energy you have left to run it in, and which adjusts your effort accordingly. It's an evolutionary development that probably arose on the African savannah when, after you'd been chasing a gazelle or some such creature for hours on end, your mind said: 'You probably want to give this a rest, it's not working out, the gazelle's faster than you – and anyway, gels and sports drinks are way off in the future and you're not wearing trainers.'

I found the theory comforting in two ways. Firstly it means that there's always more. You might be in distress and feeling that it's impossible to go faster – but that's the Central Governor talking, an essentially conservative creature, an inner Victor Meldrew, and you can ignore him, you are OK. Also, if fatigue is being mentally modulated, then there might be a way to trick it, to deceive the mind in a way that would get more out of the body.

It's impossible to describe the excitement I felt as I began to work these things out. I am not a tactician in life; I pride myself on being honest, though mostly as a hedge against having to remember anything I'm meant to have said. I'm rubbish at any form of intrigue, deception or even basic guile. Honestly, I have zero cunning, and this isn't a double bluff. I'm a truth-telling simpleton unfit for modern life. Historically, I've been resistant to even having a basic strategy. I'm a *Que sera* kind of character, throwing myself forth on the wings of fate. If it's meant to happen, then it will happen. This may be a cover for an innate laziness. You be the judge.

But changes were afoot. I can only tell you that at this stage of training I was thinking almost continuously of one very simple thing: how can I run faster?

I decided to lie to myself, to pull the wool over the eye of the Central Governor. What if, I wondered, I changed the parameters of the race I was running?

An idea had started to fester in the last couple of races, especially towards the end of the Bath half marathon. I'd noticed that there was something about the very end of races that always led to finding more energy. The finish line had an attraction to it, an inevitability rooted deep within, that made speeding up almost a given. It doesn't matter how tired you are, you can *always* summon something up. It's because you know that you're near the finish and when you reach there, that means you can stop running. And if there's one feeling better than running, it's stopping running. It's yin/yang, hot/cold, Cannon/Ball. You can't appreciate one without the other. To run for ever would be sweaty purgatory; to never run at all would be unimaginable hell; but to stop running after running is a heavenly stillness, a celestial cessation of self-inflicted torment, a sensational stasis. Pleasure chemicals ricochet through the mind as you totter down the finishing chute, hungrily replenishing the body with oxygen. I've stopped. It's over. The relief. Yes, race marshal, furnish me with medals and watery orange drink from plastic cups. Let me gulp this golden nectar (so resonant of school dinners past) and chat nonsense with my fellow travellers. Our battle is over. A minute ago we were battling for PBs; now our only interest is biscuits.

The finish, then, I had come to the conclusion, takes care of itself. It's like water down a sink, rats down a drainpipe: it's where we're all going. Given that, what would happen if I reframed the race and kidded myself that, rather than this being a 5-mile race, I was actually going to run only 4 miles? My logic was that I'd hit mid-race harder when there's a tendency to ease up, knowing that you'll be speeding up in the last mile. Maybe there's a bit of your mind in cahoots with the Central Governor and thinking: 'Fellas, we all know we'll be accelerating in the end, why not chill now? We're all mates here.'

So that's what I do, I set off fairly hard and between Miles 3 and 4 really put the hammer down (Cova! Cova!), overtaking in the process a few club mates who'd normally leave me behind. And, the last mile: I hold on. Just. It's desperate, I'm racing to every tree, furtively glancing back at every opportunity – a cardinal sin for road racing – but I keep the advancing hordes behind me at bay, and then I'm finished. It's done. Time delivered.

The digits read 00:30:25. That's 00:06:05 per mile. A breakthrough.

Calmness descends post-race, but things have changed. I've run faster than I had in ages.

Needless to say, the Central Governor is outraged. 'You told me it was a 4-mile race! I specifically spent all energy required to get to that point in the quickest time possible.'

'But, Central Governor, what about all that reserve energy that you don't tell us about?'

'Well,' splutter, splutter, 'that's none of your business. This is a relationship.'

Will he ever trust me again? No matter, I've learned a valuable lesson. There's always more in the tank and I can fool myself to get faster. I file it away in that fairly empty section of my mind called Ideas That Work, For Future Reference.

Long Sunday Run. 9 a.m. Group. 22 miles

The final piece in the highest weekly mileage jigsaw. The Long Sunday Run run, an absolute staple of any marathon training programme. For a really good marathon I'm of the notion that you need to be doing two or three runs in the 20–22 mile zone. This carries you to the very edge of the Wall, perhaps even helps you on race day to push the encounter with the Wall back a mile or so.

The 9 a.m. Sunday group is legendary in Heathside circles, a regular run consisting of mostly Group A runners. It's open to all but operates on a doctrine of No Mercy. Facebook statuses ring out the sorry tales of innocent runners who've tagged along for what they thought would be a long social run, only to be dropped ruthlessly as the pace increased towards the end and it turned into a speedy free-for-all. It's a singularly bizarre way to spend Sunday mornings, running to a state of near exhaustion, but *if* I am to have a good marathon, *if* I am realistic about the magic sub-3, I need to do this, if only the once. So I pop along at 9 as a crowd of Heathsiders gather at the foot of Archway station.

I'd done a late show at the Comedy Store in the centre of town the previous night. Normally I'd be in bed at such an ungodly hour on a Sunday, but such is the diary that this is my last chance to alight the 9 a.m. train. Late shows are chaotic and giddy experiences; you end up romping up the steps of the club into Leicester Square at 1 in the morning with a pocket full of cash, still drunk on the laughter of the mob. It's hard to sleep after this. Add to that a couple of teenagers who like to party and have a very casual relationship with house keys, and you've got a recipe right there for a fitful night's sleep.

So it's a frazzled Tonkinson who musters with the rest of them that Sunday morning. Most of them are regulars and greet me warmly, sensing new blood. One guy, Chris, is a bit older than me, hoping to do about 03:10:00 at London.

At about five minutes past the hour, we begin to jog very slowly in the direction of Highgate, hopping on and off the road haphazardly as we do so. The weather is kind this morning, clear sky, mild temperatures. The group fizzes and chats in a random, bouncing nature. I find myself next to dear old Gavin, chatting about politics and literature in quite an intelligent fashion. It feels like *The Moral Maze* on the move. We stop off at about Mile 6 in Regent's Park for a toilet break. Dominic is there with his legs reaching up to the sky; he's been training like an absolute thoroughbred. At this stage, the run is very enjoyable, civilised even. A few runners peel off to run shorter distances, but the majority are in for at least 20 miles. We run through crowds at Camden onto the towpath like a sprawling, harmless gang, splitting and rejoining like migrating birds. There must be about 20 of us in our T-shirts and shorter than short shorts, daintily picking our way through the mid-morning tourist crowd and occasional drug dealer at Camden Lock. It inspires in me a lovely sense of belonging, I feel like I'm a member of an ineffectual football firm, a slight bunch, maybe a particularly effete group of extras from the '70s classic film *Warriors*, destined never to make the final cut.

Down the path to Victoria Park. I sense the pace changing a bit. It's definitely being cranked up; hard to know whether it's a collective decision or just a by-product of being completely warmed up and in the zone. Regardless, very quickly we're clocking 7.10 miles, absurdly close to my projected race pace. My chat becomes considerably more truncated at this point, reduced to the odd breathless exclamatory comment – 'This is fast' or 'Is this normal? Help!' That sort of thing. I'm feeling the gig of the night before, I'm feeling the Yasso, the 5-mile race, the accumulation of the last few weeks; it's turning into a tough morning.

Much to my relief, the group stops at Mile 12 for a water break and to discuss plans for our immediate future. Dominic, who has been way ahead of most of us, is 'only' doing 20 miles, so he's looping off on his own for a swift 8. I'm down with the real ballers, the 22 miles or nothing gang, with five or six who are faster than me, including Gavin and Chris, and I've got the measure of him. He's heavier than me, panting quite heavily, and carries the air of a back-of-the-pack dweller. So the plan is, I'll tag along with the 22-mile lot, we'll spin out of Victoria Park, loop back down the canal, sally up to Stamford Hill and then back to Finsbury and home.

Simple. Except it isn't.

The first couple of hundred yards are fine. The group shares a bit of chat. The realisation that we are the ones this week doing the longest run imbues a short-lived bonhomie combined with a gallows humour.

Then the pace begins to nudge up a bit. Not too noticeable at first. Chris is straight off the back, but urges us on. Then another imperceptible squeeze. I was fairly comfortable on the edges of my threshold pace. As the group accelerates, I manage to stay with them for a couple of miles or so, maybe, but I stay with them for too long. I certainly get the odd surprised look at my resilience, but it's a short-lived revolution. As we drop down onto the canal, I let them go, and watch as they slowly but inevitably pull further and further away on the long run back to Highgate. I sort of know the way home and am aware that under no circumstances do I want to slow the pack down. This is a training run, not childcare, and I've lived in London for 20 years.

I plod on alone, all enthusiasm suddenly punctured. The excesses of the week have really taken hold now. To all intents and purposes this run is over. Very quickly I'm fantasising about getting back to the car, sinking into the bath, submerging myself in that hot soapy water with a massive cup of tea on the side and a pile of choc 'n' nut cookies. Maybe a long kip this afternoon. That's it. A long kip, then I can look at the week's training and delight in my achievements. But still, this pain. The next mile and the one after that. Please Lord, bring this sorry affair to an end. How long now? 5 miles, 4? I hear Chris coming up behind me. He's moving comically slowly yet absurdly seems to be reeling me in. Very soon he pulls alongside. We run together for a minute; it's a weird feeling of mutual embarrassment to be running at such a snail-like pace, though naturally at this moment, Chris is on a faster pace. There's no point even trying to run together; we're both locked into a pitiful survival struggle, recognising in one another a mutual exhaustion.

'I'm just trying to keep running. However slowly,' I offer, by way of explanation.

To his credit, he makes no pretence that what we are doing is in any way enjoyable. 'It's good training for the day. This is what it will be like – just plodding along. You know the way?'

'I'll be fine.'

At that, he's away, hobbling painfully off, moving so slowly – which means I'm even slower, stumbling around faintly alien streets. From above, it must look like the most pathetic chase scene ever witnessed. I keep him in the distance for a while, more as a guide than anything, but soon the effort this involves becomes too great and I am rendered completely adrift from my club mates, rudderless and at risk of being totally lost. What gives it all a slightly surreal nature is that this occurs slap bang in the middle of Stamford Hill, an area very popular with the Orthodox Jewish community, the largest Hasidic community in Europe. So it's large families and huge side curls and many startled glances as I weave my merry way among them this Sunday morning. It's like being on the set of *Fiddler on the Roof*. In my confused and exhausted state and many miles from home, I briefly wonder whether it might be possible, and easier, to just stop running, relocate and live among them. I've always loved the Jewish people: the sense of community, the wisdom of the Torah, the importance of the family, the beautiful rituals of worship.

Would Ra mind if I just gave her a shout? 'Pack the bags, we're moving to Stamford Hill! Phone that bloke from New York back, I'm learning Hebrew. We're getting a Volvo. Start looking at halls for Rudy's bar mitzvah. If I were a rich man!'

It's not to be. To be honest, I don't know if they would accept me this morning, a ponderous, sweaty Gentile. I keep running. I always keep running, but it's not a pretty sight. Somehow I make my way back to Finsbury Park and from there, back on home turf, I know I'm barely 2 miles away from the car. Just down the Parkland Way, plodding – like Chris said, just plodding on. Last on the day but towards the end of the biggest training week of my life. In a lonely hole of my own digging but continuing none the less, crafting the mind, training that state of pure obstinacy that I feel sure I'll need on the day. Up the hill back to the oasis of my car, everyone long gone.

I have done all the training I could physically do.

Three weeks to go.

18

Pantsgate

But beware, amid such continual sacrifice there is fallout, in often surprising areas.

Fairly soon, after I'd taken on the mantle of hero, I went for a massage two doors down from me. The hero's body must be supple and lithe as opposed to stiff and robotic. Increased mileage and very little stretching had truncated the muscles and made running more effort than necessary. So I rang Claire.

Claire is a trained sports therapist, a lovely person combining a smooth sense of authority with a vaguely hippyish vibe that gives you everything you'd want from a massage. She will douse your body in hot oils and apply stones in just the right places; her professional fingers will loosen and cajole your muscles back to life; you can literally feel pockets of tissue dissolve at her touch, leaving you supple and refreshed upon departure. So it was Claire I called halfway through the training process one Wednesday afternoon in early April. Claire, who lives just two doors down from me, who laid me down and asked me to disrobe to my shorts while she lit a candle, and it was Claire whose innocent hands were subjected to the appalling surface of my cresting testicle as the room echoed to the sounds of whale music.

As I said, fallout.

To be clear, I'd not gone there with the intention of initiating testicle–hand contact. We had gathered in good faith on that clear, if slightly grey afternoon. Claire was there to practise her profession. I was keen to ease my stiff legs. The problem was that the area causing me most problems was my inner thigh/groin region. The other problem was my shorts.

Now, I'm a naturally shy person around matters of the body. You will not see me parading naked round the changing rooms. I'm a furtive changer, a private citizen with no desire to inflict my genitals on anyone other than my wife or, occasionally, my kids for comic effect. On the rare occasions I've been massaged, I've taken good care to wear an all-encompassing solid pair of pants. This particular afternoon I went double bubble: shorts and pants. The running shorts lacked an inner brief, which could cause much kerfuffle in the undercarriage. To counteract this, I had hastily put on a pair of black pant trunks for reinforcements. You would have thought this would leave me feeling extremely secure in the area that mattered. And at first it did; I whipped off my tracksuit top and bottoms with aplomb and lay face down on the massage table, putting my face into the little circle designed for such occasions. It was at that moment I felt a slightly pinched sensation in my groin. No biggie, I just slightly adjusted the position as Claire got to work, beginning with my lower calves and feet, and gradually unlocking the legs. The upper groin had borne the brunt of the increased mileage, but Claire took a holistic view and worked around the area with a trained but gentle insistence. Perhaps it was the ease of her touch, the light of the candles and the hypnotic sounds of the whale music, but very soon I was semi-conscious, surrendering to the experience. It was only when I was roused from my semi-slumber and prompted to turn over onto my back that I glimpsed potential problems.

On a very simple level, I'd worn the wrong set of pants.

Like most people (!?), I have a highly variable quality of pants to hand in the cupboard. Although long past the need for 'pulling pants', I have a variety of fairly fashionable, designer, trunk-style, tight-fitting garments that would pass muster if suddenly subjected to public scrutiny. Then I have the second-tier pants, old boxer shorts and over-tight Y-fronts that I'll pull on for a day ligging round the house. In among these lurks a rogue third tier: a motley crew of damaged, frayed-at-the-edges pants, in some cases severely damaged, gusset-less monstrosities that should have no place in any wardrobe. Pants that make you think: *Are these even pants? What purpose do they possibly serve?* Of course, I should throw these out – but being a bit of a hoarder, I rarely do. The problem is, these pants often look, upon a perfunctory perusal, as if they may be normal, black, decent trunk pants. It's only upon wearing them that you sense the abandoned dangle of the utterly useless undergarment. In day-to-day life this is not a problem; you feel an irritation as nether parts brush up repeatedly against whatever trouser you're wearing, but it's no biggie. It's a fleeting, private sensation.

As I flipped myself over in Claire's front room, I felt that I was about to go public. I could feel the testicles breaking free of their unruly mesh, threatening to peek out of the shorts in an audacious but disturbing bid for freedom. Physics helped their cause, the natural flow of fabric riding ever so slightly up my upper thigh as I leaned back. I didn't know what to do. I was in the middle of a flow experience and didn't want to break the solemn but healing atmosphere. I consoled myself with the thought that she might have encountered this before, the rogue testicle issue. Anyway, it felt rude to ask. For the minute there was no real need to mention it. The shorts still cradled the errant testes. But it was no good, the uneasy truce could not hold. Here was the perfect storm: the shorts, the pants, the temperature of the room, the relaxation of the massage. On another day my testes might have retreated into my body. But today in the warmth, my jewels lounged confidently, swinging with every circular sweep as Claire's hands made a beeline for my inner thigh.

Escape felt inevitable.

I inhaled sharply upon each swoop as my scrotum teased the edge of the shorts and then, after one extremely close forage, as Claire's hands swept back down the thigh, my right testicle made an appearance. Not the whole thing. Glancing down, I witnessed just a strangulated half-moon. Like a very small baby's head, mottled but alive, peering into the light.

I made a noise, a restrained 'Ttssh' of warning, but it was too late. The whole thing happened too quickly, and Claire grazed it on the upsweep. I felt the faintest of nips from her nail and yelped involuntarily, bucking forwards as I did so. From a different angle it might well have looked like the clichéd happy ending, instead of the disaster that it was.

I manoeuvred myself off the massage table, apologising profusely. To be fair, Claire seemed unfazed. It was, we agreed, one of those things. Mortified, I tucked myself in, vigorously mashing my scrotum back into as tight a corner as I could.

There were 10 minutes left. We are both pleased to report the massage passed from that point without incident.

Note to self: Chuck out old pants!

Mile 18. Isle of Dogs to Canary Wharf. Crossing over

Goal time – 02:02:15. Actual time – 02:02:24

This is not a particularly salubrious area for passing from one dimension into another, but there seems little choice in the matter. I've been running hard for just over two hours now so, see you on the other side, I'm going under. That is to say, I pronounce myself officially knackered.

Banjaxed.

Kiboshed.

Spent.

The mad happy dash that made no sense at all at Mile 16 makes even less sense now; in fact, all sense is receding. I am knocking on the door of the Wall, the door is opening. I am no longer pure light, I am heavy and daft, slurping thirstily on a bottle of water, squirting it on my head, neck, the back of my hamstrings and then hurling it off to the gutter. I could easily unravel here.

Help me, please. Throw me a life raft.

My eyes ferret out into the crowd, I'm looking for faces in the throng to connect with, anything at all that would give me a scrap of energy. Up to now, I've been taking them for granted. Now I need them. And yet, just as I need their concrete encouragement, their voices are blending. My senses are going a bit, narrowing. It's the old Central Governor. He's husbanding resources to where they are needed.

Forwards. Ever forwards. Let that be the focus. Loosen the body if you can. Push. Push.

In terms of sheer numbers, the bodies by the side of the road are getting more numerous, packed closer together. We are reaching the business end of the day. Comments are sharper, more directed. There is an urgency coming off them. I need to stay in my race. I could lose myself in their anxious faces.

Think form. Cova. Light steps. Onwards. Push, push.

And yet, much as I try, I am bleeding out into them. The noise is irresistible, it is penetrating my focus. To do well, to succeed today, I must use them. I must harness it. Their positivity can feed me. No swearing at innocent kids today – or anytime for that matter.

The trees love the rain.

Up to now my pace has been perfect. That could change very easily. At this stage, there are absolutely no guarantees. I've been here before – in 2005, in York. I'm older now, wiser, but possibly weaker and with 13 more years of accumulated wear and tear in the system, the untallied but continuous grind that is our lives. The travel, all that sugar and bread, late night cheeseathons, Two Bottle Sundays, therapy, the exhaustion and exhilaration and sheer energy expenditure of three kids. A toll has been taken, charges have been administered. I'm older, and for a second I'm really feeling it. In fact, if you want to see how you're going to look in 20 years' time, have a look at your race photo 18 miles into a marathon. I know, frightening.

But the race must continue, this saga. This ultimate test that no one cares about but me.

There are two things going on at once.

I am totally concentrating on the run – and yet absolutely dependent on the crowd's support. It's a symbiotic relationship between the runners and watchers. Their shouts and exhortations are lifting me up, our effort encourages them. As I tire and my senses lose their acuity, the voices echo and bounce into my head. We are beginning to fuse. It's a phenomenon that has been described by psychologists as 'participation mystique' – a process by which spectators become indistinguishable from the object that they are viewing. They are psychologically projecting over the runners to such a strong level that it's tantamount to a partial identity.

You get it at the football, when those key moments happen. That split second when the crowd's desire and anticipation find perfect form in the player's action, that incredible brilliant moment of realisation as the net ripples.

Goal! An incredible *Yes!*

Normal boundaries dissolve. It's an eternal, white-hot moment of supernatural clarity. Even the players feel it, often jumping into the crowds themselves. It is a second when we realise a conscious unity with all living beings – or, at least, the winning team. To watch a mass marathon is slightly different, you are being exposed to thousands of stories, an ever-changing kaleidoscope of projection. Every runner is attractive to each spectator for a variety of personal reasons. Runner upon runner, with all their hopes, dreams, motivations. For those watching, the runners' struggles become their struggles in life. The runners' pain, their pain. For a day, the marathon runners are living symbols of the triumphs and disasters in life, men and women of all ages, backgrounds, abilities, shapes and sizes, heroes all. They are being cheered, harangued, laughed at, urged on. It is a festival, a freak show, an outpouring, a celebration.

It's very London: English yet global.

In the pack, the atmosphere is more restrained. Physically there has been a thinning out. Although all day has been spent running in close proximity to others, there is more than enough space now, and mental attrition has exacerbated the distance between us. Camaraderie between runners has dissipated. That's not to say it doesn't exist; it's just that there's no energy on tap to display it. Survival mode is fully operational. We can no longer help each other. Up to now, there has been the odd word between us. Now silence reigns.

I've got one gel left. Drinks are no problem, but my muscles protest lustily with each step. I'm into the last third of the run. That's one way of looking at it: three thirds, each of an hour. I've thought about this a lot. I've worked on my head, my will, tried to strengthen it. Told myself to get tough. It's worked; I feel massive resolve and yet there's something else happening as well. I'm in an odd state of limbo at Mile 18, almost a sadness.

I'll try to explain.

As I desperately try to maintain pace, I know that if I am to do this, if I am to beat three hours and lay this thing to rest, it is going to be without doubt the hardest thing I've done physically in my life. Melodramatic certainly, but this is a truth that I am living at this very second. Of course, I've chosen this freely, I accept it, but – if I extrapolate this bone-crushing tiredness onwards for another 8 miles, there's no sugarcoating it, this will be horrendous.

And yet, bizarrely, this realisation coexists with the knowledge that I am utterly determined to do it. There's just no way I'm letting all that training go to waste. Today is the day, I'm leaving it all out. Nothing left at the end of it. This gets done.

But, to be honest, it's also a bit weird because these two thoughts join to form a little thought bubble that floats above my running body. *Who does this kind of thing? What does it say about my life that I have to take this on, create such unwarranted drama?*

There is a crushing weariness at the inevitability of the physical pain I've signed up for, of which I am guaranteeing more with every step. It's almost a misery provoked by nothing more than the realisation that this is the kind of human I am.

It's a moment of spiking depression, a dark mile of the soul, probably prompted by fatigue. I know that I am going to propel mercilessly ever forward into this. I know I've created a map of meaning within myself that will allow no surrender to it – but I'm not proud, I don't feel heroic. To be honest, I feel a bit stupid. *Why can't I just come and watch ... or do other events? I used to play football; that was alright, apart from the fighting. I like football. Tennis. I love tennis. Just do that more. What is this? What am I playing at? I could coach kids. That's it. I could start a kids' football team in a deprived area. Charitable giving. That's the way forward. This is a selfish, murky enterprise.*

And then Dominic passes me, off to my left in a group of four or five runners. Heathsiders have popped up throughout the day, like a race within a race. The deep blue sash, the yellow and red. It's been a comfort. A reminder that, amid the madness and the heightened spectacle of it all, it's just a race; we're all just running, like we have been doing together all winter.

I catch him out of the corner of my eye. I'd been expecting to see him at some point or other. I'd fantasised about reaching him as we ran down the Embankment for the last mile together, coming home down The Mall in unison, cracking the three hours in victory. I wanted us to do this together. But for now he is ever so slowly passing me. I don't even say hello. To be fair, he might not have seen me. And to shout out would have taken too much effort for both of us. He seems locked in, running smoothly but just starting to look laboured, as we all are. After all, this hurts, and there seems no end to it.

Sounds and sight are getting a bit hazy. I don't know what running hard for this long does to consciousness, but it's easy to get confused. That's why you need a clear plan. For this brief passage I am totally concerned with maintaining pace. I've got ideas for later on. Now it's a holding phase.

It's like the scene in *The Perfect Storm* where the crew bed down for the night as they approach the rumbling mass of dark clouds before the calamity. We are going in to something. We've prepared but have no idea how or if we can get through it. The usefulness of rational thought and tactics is receding with every step. This experience will ask more of us than maybe we would like. I watch Dominic's graceful style slowly edging into the distance, merging with the vests and shorts, the arms and legs in front of me.

Eighteen miles done and dusted. My legs are still moving, but I am falling off, off and away – into a liminal space.

From now on, the battle is internal.

19

York Marathon. There are things we don't know we don't know

The marathon is primarily a physical challenge. Of that, there is no doubt. Simple, practical steps can be taken to increase the chances of running a strong marathon and not being rendered a babbling tearful wreck by the Wall.

In terms of diet, carb-loading is a must. All the stuff that experts tell you to eat in moderation is sanctioned by running long distances. Bread. Potatoes. Pasta. Lots of lovely carbs for the three or four days before the marathon – not necessarily in terms of quantity but in terms of proportion. It's easy to put on weight during this period, you're tapering, which means you're running less, expanding less energy. You don't want to turn up on race day bloated and gaseous, feeling heavy and inert. No. You want light, buoyant, yet strong. To get this, just eat less protein generally and add brown rice, quinoa or a baked potato (sweet potatoes are best). For the last few days, I'm eating good carbs with every meal. This fills your legs with the sustaining magic of glycogen, the energy-providing chemical your muscles need to delay fatigue, the energy for your motor. I don't know the science – just do it. It's a laugh having pasta pesto for breakfast.

On the morning of the race, you'll find what suits you. Nothing too taxing to the system. Bananas. Bit of cereal perhaps. I got the malt loaf tip from Vassos, and that works for me.

Training is simple once you've decided to just do it. Running is the answer to all your problems. Lots of it at varying paces and distances. You're trying to log in your race pace as the default setting in your body. For me, that's 06:52 per mile; you may be faster or slower. In any state you want to feel you can crank out race pace. The only way to do this is to get to know it intimately, by running faster than race pace, slower, bang on it. Train your body and mind to know it absolutely. And then three or four runs in the over 20-mile range. Nice and steady – and, if possible, speeding up or at least putting in more effort towards the end. This trains the body and mind to keep pushing when exhausted (that default again). Then, when you finish the long run, chug a sports drink to replace lost salts and energy. Scoff a banana or two. You've got a window of about 40 minutes to replenish the body. If you can, try and stretch here as well. Anything to avoid cramps and tightness. When I'm in deep training mode, I like to do long runs on no food at all. This helps the body utilise fuel better while running and also helps lose weight. Throw on another sweat shirt as well if you're feeling particularly masochistic, but don't go easy on the water. Hydration is good!

As runners, we are all a dynamic experiment of one: mixing and matching methods. What works for one runner might not work for another, particularly in terms of training load. You might have to adapt to a change in lifestyle. The most important thing is continuous, uninterrupted training; there's a momentum to the weeks and months. That means if we feel too tired or a bit under par one day, then we ease off, so we can run the next day. We read, listen to others, learn. We apply techniques and measure results on race day.

York Marathon, six months before London, was the pinnacle of my purely physical approach, the nexus of all my accumulated knowledge. I'd trained with self-awareness, lost weight, done the long runs.

Experts advise having three goals for each race. This takes into account the slings and arrows of outrageous fortune. You might turn up on the day and find the weather is appalling. You might fall over, get cramp. It's nice to have a range of options to realign yourself with if circumstances change on the day.

So then, for York, three goals it was:

First off: you need a *perfectly acceptable* goal. A time you'd expect to achieve that would give you satisfaction. At York, this was to beat my PB of 03:09:42. I was much fitter than I'd ever been before. Surely this was in the bag.

Then you want a *this is actually a good run* goal. A time that would represent real, tangible progress. For this race, less than 03:05:00. That would mean surpassing my PB by over four minutes. A massive leap forward. Doable given my current physical state at the time.

Finally, of course, you need a *shoot to the moon, eat your pants, phone your dead grandad* mind-blowing achievement. A run that would send you back down the M1 to home giddy with joy, fuelled by the fumes of pure triumph.

You know this by now. Sub-3.

Physically, I felt this was on the cards. Mentally, I was also starting to sort my head out. I'd found a little bubble of angry joy inside me, which I was tapping into while competing. It was like a well deep inside me. The harder I ran, the more energy I found – within reason. I hadn't stumbled upon an infinite store, just a new reserve. An abundance hitherto undiscovered.

And I felt calm. This is important too. The more you train, the more you read, the more you understand of the event, the calmer you'll feel on the day and the less energy you'll disperse on all the unnecessary stuff. And of that there is loads at most marathons: the expos, the registration, the arrival on the day, the dropping your bags off. It can all conspire to drain your mental reserves.

You need to sail through this, and the more prepared you are, the less it will affect you. If you want a good run, you must visualise it all. Arrival. Warming up. Walking to the start. The last few minutes before the start. By visualising, you've planted seeds in your mind, and now this feels like a part you're playing. Nothing will faze you. That's important.

At the start in York I saw a case study in pre-marathon panic. A young lad, around 19 or 20, appeared 10 metres in front of us. He had all the gear: the heart monitors, the compression socks, ultra-modern vest and shorts, chunky Garmin. With 10 minutes to go he began feverishly stretching and exhaling in a manner more befitting a competitor at the Hunger Games. His eyes manically darted around his surroundings as he repeatedly touched his toes, alternating with vigorously jogging on the spot, twisting his upper body, sipping energy drinks and pouring water over his head despite it being very mild conditions. It was all a bit extra. I know I'm old school, but let's keep it simple, and let's not forget, we're only running here. This is a very natural activity that we have done since childhood. All this paraphernalia has only arisen because we enjoy it so much. Let us proceed without fear. Ironically, this guy needed an inner Snoop to help him. A shame because he looked extremely fit, his muscles rippled with a feline elasticity, he seemed to have no fat upon his person. He'd obviously done the training, but he was leaking mental energy all over the place. The mind was galloping away with him, his race being ruined right at this very moment with every grotesque overstretch. It was like watching a teenager doing double shots of vodka on the way to a party. Keep your powder dry. In your overexcited state, you're missing the moment. Nothing's happened yet.

What I was starting to work out in York was that a big part of the marathon is about how and when to disperse your mental and physical energy. Keep it for when you need it, beyond 20 miles.

York was a good run.

Very quickly I found a smallish group of four or five runners who were all operating at sub-3 pace. We talked and ambled along together quite happily through Yorkshire streets. I felt blissfully happy at this stage; it reminded me very strongly of childhood, training with Scarborough Harriers on the clifftops. There was a sense of homecoming about it, the friendliness and easy banter, none of the tension of London with its mad dash at every water station and the slight mania, at least in the early stages, around personal space. You could run freely at York in your own little pocket, unencumbered, which frankly was a relief. I was steadily becoming aware of quite intense issues around fluid retention.

Hydration is crucial to a decent marathon. As with many things, it's something that people tend to obsess about unnecessarily. 'What shall I drink?' people ask, as if it's some great mystery. How often? How much? Just drink beforehand till you're not thirsty, and have a little often during the marathon itself. Find your way with energy drinks. I have one a half hour before and little sips during the race. It's that experiment thing again. Some swear by coffee as a legal aid to performance. I've had limited success with this. The main thing is, don't overdrink (or overthink). Don't have a litre at every water station, or you'll overfill. And if you get thirsty, don't stress, bruv, it's the body doing what the body does. Just have a drink and don't feel thirsty anymore. Chill out! (All runs change in very hot conditions. Then you need to drink more and assess very carefully. Take 10 minutes off your goal time and look after yourself.)

At York I'd done the carb-loading but hadn't quite fine-tuned it. I felt slightly overweight and bloated as I lined up. I don't know whether this was a factor – maybe it put strain on my bladder; I don't know how inner mechanics work – but all I can say is that every time I had a drink during the race to quench thirst it was accompanied a minute down the road with an overwhelming desire to urinate. An irresistible urge. So then, a conundrum. I'm on for a fast time, yet I have this recurring, ahem, situation.

Let's talk tactics. At most races of this nature, the route is lined with portaloos. These are quick and easy to use. I think York had some, though less so out in the countryside, which the course spreads out into wonderfully. There were also numerous hedgerows or areas of woodland to nip into, and spend a penny in a subtle manner. We've all seen it and done it, both pre-race and during. It's semi-accepted that legions of runners will be relieving themselves on every available bit of space on every available surface. No problem.

Only it is, because I'm on for a good time. Every pit stop is at least a minute. I'm needing one every few miles. I can't lose seven or eight minutes, there goes my PB. So... I devised, and would like to copyright, the Tonkinson Manoeuvre: doing it on the run.

Now, I'm not actually advocating this. I share it in a spirit of truth, and it's not ideal and definitely not a situation to be wished for – *but*, if you are desperate to go and keen to maintain pace, it is possible. I like to combine it with a water station or, at least, close to a water station. What you do is you slow down, pick up a bottle or a sponge and then combine the act of urination with the general splashing about that happens at such times anyway. I pour water everywhere at water stations, all over, including my upper thighs. It's not too much of a deviation to squeeze a sponge down the front of your shorts while you let nature run its course. Everyone's getting on with their own thing, it's not really that embarrassing. I mean, it can be. It depends on your mentality. I confess, it was only a bit shameful in retrospect. Once I'd got my head round it and accepted what I was going to do – which was, let's not beat around the bush, pee my pants – it was a pleasurable relief. I found myself almost looking forward to it. Speeding up slightly to the water station, picking up a bottle, easing up to the side of the road, sipping my bottle and keeping half a bottle or so for the water-urination fusion. Then, the letting go. Once started, not at all bad. It felt brutally animalistic: hot, horse-like and perfectly natural. A manifestation of my desire to run fast, which made total sense.

I've never had the problem to this extent before or since, but York was a kind of madness. I was simultaneously thirsty and bursty, so I did what was necessary.

It was only post-race that I realised how unusual it is to do this. Euphoria had dampened my memory. Upon finishing, I completely forgot the toilet dramas of the race. In fact, I chatted and shared stories from the front like a perfectly well-adjusted member of society. It was only halfway through the massage, as a chatty volunteer working on my upper thighs pulled up short and came to a sudden halt with an appalled expression, that I realised the after-effects of my morning's bladder abandon. To put it simply, my shorts smelled shall we say fruity, an aroma that had deepened in complexity and depth post-race. I had ignored its faint strain, but there on the table, it was unmistakable, like a baby's nappy. I levered myself off the massage table with a look of apology and made haste for the nearest changing booth.

The race itself had been a corker. All the training paid off. I sailed through 20 miles, and barrelled through 22 miles, running a mile in 00:06:23; but then the Wall crashed the party, and any hopes of a sub-3 were strangled. I slowed markedly over the last miles. The three-goal thing had given me an out, though, and I grasped on to it wholeheartedly. I ran 03:03:52 that day. A big step forward. Huge, in fact.

The finishers' enclosure was bouncing with Yorkshire bonhomie and sheer big-hearted fun. I chatted like an infant to anyone and everyone who'd listen. The bloke running for his dad who had his head in his hands, crying from pure relief. Several fans of the podcast who seemed as excited to meet me as I was to meet them. For that day the running was over; we could eat and drink to our hearts' content. Collate our victories, lament our defeats, plan for the future, bank the knowledge and feel this utter relief at stopping.

But deep down, I knew it was an underperformance. Sub-3 was there for me that day, low-hanging fruit, but it had eluded me.

Physically, I had learned everything I needed to do. Mentally, I was making huge strides. I was feeling competitive, bullish even. Dispersal of energy was being used in an intelligent fashion. I was leaving no stone unturned in my quest for a marathon beginning with the digit 2. I was pissing myself on the run, for goodness sake!

But still, as the post-race buzz faded, as shorts were changed and trains boarded back down to London, I knew I had short-changed myself. The fruit cake and tea was sticking in my craw a little on the £15 First Class Sunday upgrade. I knew that at my age there was only a small window of opportunity left to join the ranks of the sub-3, and that window was closing.

Sub-3. Sub fucking 3.

In a world of marginal gains, I was missing out.

I needed a miracle to push me over the edge. I needed a mantra.

20

Meaningful mantras. Rudeness

I was introduced to the concept of mantras while watching the classic Woody Allen comedy *Annie Hall*. There's an iconic scene in the film where Jeff Goldblum is on the phone to his therapist in an achingly cool LA party, confessing that he'd forgotten his.

Mantras were thus established in my mind as the ridiculous affectations of a decadent, glib culture. Growing up in the '80s, I saw them all around me, mostly from the world of advertising. From 'Beans meanz Heinz' to Nike imploring me to 'Just do it', pithy phrases abounded and, on the whole, were trying to sell me something that I didn't particularly want. (Though to this day I retain a penchant for Heinz and I'm wearing a Nike T-shirt as I write.) As the 21st century bedded in, mantras became woven into the fabric of society, blending with mission statements and popularised by huge corporations. Facebook's Mark Zuckerberg wanted to 'move fast and break things', Google set out to 'do no evil', Apple tried to 'think different'. In my prolonged flirtation with self-help literature, I'd gained an understanding of the power of words, how the phrases we use can shape our minds over time. Self-talk, as Gavin said, is very important. All speech must be monitored closely; it resonates through eternity. The messages we send out to the world are crucial. (*This is a great book, an inspiring yet comic tale worth recommending to runners and non-runners alike.*)

The things we repeatedly say about ourselves and others are significant. I'd just never taken the final leap into using a mantra to help me run faster.

No surprises there; I've usually been resistant to new information or ideas in my life. Some would call me a Luddite. (If you don't know what Luddite is, google it. If you don't know how to do that, you are one.) I remember having a heated chat with some mates in the mid '90s, arguing vehemently against the concept of email. It would not, I was sure, ever catch on.

'But what about the obvious benefits of convenience?' they argued. 'The ease of communication?'

'People prefer the intimacy of a handwritten letter,' I insisted. 'Pen and paper. Stamps. Receiving an envelope through the post. In fact, let's go the whole hog and buy a fountain pen.'

I genuinely believed this. In my mind it was something about the sanctity of communication.

Wherever there's a zeitgeist, you can find me limping along several years behind, hot and bothered, not really understanding. Even now, I'm massively resistant to modernity.

Social media for instance? Evil.

Wireless headphones? Dangerous and unnecessary.

Give me a minute and I will mount a sturdy riposte to the advent of driverless cars. *They'll never catch on. People like driving.*

Basically, if it had been down to me, mankind would still be living wild on the African savannah. No, I'd say, I see no need for the wheel. We're perfectly happy walking, thank you very much. If we start wheeling around all over the place, we'll get lost. And stop rubbing those sticks together, it'll cause a fire. Never do that again!

Likewise, with running. Everything I have learned has been at a glacial pace. In some ways this is the way of learning itself. Unless you experience it, advice makes no sense. If I'd embraced what more experienced runners had told me years ago, I would have saved myself a lot of bother. For years, I thought the halfway mark in the marathon was at Mile 13. Once I discovered it was, in fact, at Mile 20, the marathon became much easier. I've had a similar relationship with gels. I used to see them as a tool for the feeble-minded, the newcomer. They didn't have them in my day in the '80s, so what use could they possibly be now? Evidently, a lot of use. Especially when you're trying to fuel a marathon.

So when marathon veterans sidled up to me post-training, proselytising about mantras, my eyes glazed over as they do when I'm chatting to a Jehovah's Witness. It just wasn't what I wanted to sign up for. Then I began to think a bit more clearly.

York should have seen a sub-3. I was on pace for miles and miles. Then came the fade. Part of this was because I hadn't mentally prepared properly. My hopes had been too vague. I needed to be detailed and definite as to what I actually wanted. For me, in this instance, I also realised that three goals was just too confusing. Chaotic times need simple messages.

It's easy to underestimate how lousy you're going to feel at Mile 20, how disorientating it can become. It's bedlam, biblically bad, purgatorial. I've seen people cramp up suddenly, collapsing to the ground, emergency services scurrying to assist. I've witnessed runners rip off their vest in disgust, argue with police officers, projectile vomit. It's mayhem. In that confused state, as you gingerly negotiate this fragile space between will and wilting, progress and chaos, you need a light, a clear message to think of, to take your hand and lead you through the darkness. This is where a mantra comes in. A short phrase that resonates. A collection of words that, when repeated privately, inspire feelings of fortitude and resilience.

It can be very simple. In Dean Karnazes' classic book *Ultramarathon Man: Confessions of an All-Night Runner*, we find Dean understandably in trouble, somewhere near Mile 99 of a 100-mile run. Distraught, exhausted and abandoned, he lies washed up on the street, bereft of any energy, completely broken, so near and yet so existentially far from the finish. He is being watched by a quizzical couple in a car. Then, from nowhere, a phrase pops up, one that he finds himself saying out loud:

I can.

They both stared at me. With even more resilience in my voice, I repeated 'I can!'

They blinked at me, but the husband played along, bellowing heartily.

'Yes. You can!'

I don't think it's that much of a plot spoiler to say that he found the energy from somewhere to stand up, shake loose and run the last mile, even speeding up near the end. He did. He definitely did. But it was that very simple phrase – *I can* – that unlocked the energy allowing him to do so. An energy that he had no idea existed. We are capable of much more than we imagine – in life and in running – but we get comfortable. That's a sign of our success as a society, of course. Let's enjoy the comfort of modern life, the plethora of entertainment options, ease of travel, the availability of food and furnishings. It is an achievement to be celebrated. So let's Netflix and chill, pop that Nutribullet on and sink into our fine elephant cotton pillows, but let's not delude ourselves: it's only when we find ourselves in the most desperate of situations that we find out who we are.

National treasure Sophie Raworth found herself in the back of an ambulance at Mile 16 of her first marathon. She was dehydrated, bleeding and unconscious. After being tended to by medical staff for 40 minutes, you'd assume that would be it for the day. Go to hospital, maybe? Phone a relative? Nope. Despite being urged not to continue, she ignored their advice, jumped out and finished the race. I don't know what roused her, but that impulse, that decision to go again must, I'm sure, have paved the way for a nourishing and flourishing career in running. Ten years later she's run multiple marathons, ultras, marathons des sables. All, I would argue, prompted by that singular and self-defining choice: *This is not how my day ends. I'm not staying here. I'm off.*

Mantras differ, they are unique to each individual. The only criterion is that it has to connect with you as a runner, a person in the world. To construct one that's meaningful is an extremely useful exercise. It forces you to think about your inner motivation for running, the primal impulse. It strikes to the core of your identity. It might be positive, it could be meditative or more elemental, direct; rude even. All it has to do is work. It's a deeply personal thing, a code to unlock your potential. You need a mantra that brings together your conscious and subconscious mind, a phrase that unites the warring voices in your head. Get it right, and it will lift you in the toughest of moments.

I've always favoured a short one, but again, lengths differ. Rob Deering, my Running Commentary friend, struggled for years to get the right tone. Eventually he settled on (and I don't think he'll mind me sharing; he put it on the podcast): *All Lights Are Green, All Systems Are Go.* To my ears, it sounded comically over-elaborate, but the more we talked about it, the more it made sense. He's a fan of sci-fi and it's a quotation from *Capricorn One*, a film he loves. More importantly it echoed Rob's feeling while running: the idea of the body as a highly functioning machine, a smooth system. Dynamically it also dovetails with his running style – metronomic, contained, efficient. In conclusion, the whole thing works a treat, and it's helped propel his running to the next level.

In the last couple of weeks before London, as training became less taxing, I had time to think about this, to really get it right. Physically, the lights were green; mentally, I needed a strong mantra.

In the last few races, as my fitness developed and speed increased, I had noticed I had been getting a bit snarlier. I don't mean literally; I just mean I had been starting to feel a bit more like I used to when I played football on Hackney Marshes, more blatantly competitive. Running had lost its spiritual edge for me – or maybe refined it. When I had rediscovered running throughout my adult life, it had been primarily a spiritual/psychological balm, a meditative jaunt through nature to ease my troubled soul. This had worked and would always be the bedrock of my connection to it. But as the sub-3 marathon grew in my mind and took shape as a real and proper goal, my attitude started to change a bit, my will started to harden. I wasn't running this race just to share a day with like-minded souls. I was in it to win it. Not the whole thing, obviously. But *my* day. This day that I had created with me at the centre had clear parameters of victory and defeat, and I was aiming for these without shame. I was telling everyone, I'm going for this. I'M GOING TO RUN A MARATHON IN UNDER THREE HOURS. This was part of the strategy. Every time I said it out loud, I was creating a world where this was possible.

I knew on one level that this was all preposterous. I was aware of the cosmic joke of it all, aware that it really wasn't of any significance – but to do it, I had to invest, I had to create meaning, had to consider it as very important while knowing it wasn't. It's a game, a lovely game round intent and achievement. By seeing it as a game, we can enjoy it more. (I've always loved sports and games for this reason, with their clear parameters, as opposed to the messy business of actual life.) The whole experience, the grind of the training, the dietary sacrifices, the mental tactics. I was creating a highly personal measure of me as a person: the sub-3. I ran the game. I created the rules. I controlled the experiment, this harmless game that I was nevertheless determined to win!

It's that old self-help saying, isn't it: *If you've got a strong enough why, you'll accept any how.* If I could work out, or even create a story that was deep enough for me, I could do the training necessary, accept the pain on the day.

In chatting casually to various sports psychologists, I became aware of the advantages of using anger as a motivating tool, the idea of positive rage. Looking around, at heroes, real sporting heroes of my youth, I saw that their stories were not all sweetness and light. The best, the very best, often seemed to be driven by a deep sense of vengeance. As a 14-year-old I stayed up into the wee small hours to watch Sebastian Coe win gold in the Olympic 1500 metres at Los Angeles after a long battle with illness the previous year. Now, Coe is a well-spoken individual, known for his gentlemanly conduct, but when he crossed the line, beating Steve Cram in the process, his first action was not to wave cheerily to the crowd, or even fall to his knees in joy and supplication. It was to turn with fire in his eye and direct a stream of invective towards the press box. Likewise, when Ali beat Foreman in Zaire (the famous rope-a-dope fight described by Norman Mailer in his superb book *The Fight*), much of his press conference was spent lambasting the press and his critics therein. Watch it on YouTube: 'All of my critics crawl...' Both men had created a narrative where in some way the world was against them, and so winning assumed a massive importance; it was a battle between them and the world.

Irrational? Certainly. Ever so slightly unhinged? Absolutely, but mightily effective, in the scheme of things.

Now, this was not an option open to me, using the media as a motivational tool. I'd been too lucky in life and obviously not talented enough as a runner to attract the slings and arrows of the press. Also, to be pedantic, my motives were never about beating anyone else. For me, running, especially in the marathon, is an activity where we compete not to beat other people but to get the best of ourselves. If I run hard, you run hard, then I run harder, etc. It's a shared thing, we're helping each other.

But having said that, I saw something in the antics of vastly more successful types that might be genuinely available to us all if we are willing to delve into our psyches for motivational nuggets.

I looked back to the days when I started running. Thought of that young, determined whippersnapper strapping up his Dunlops and taking to the streets, or sneaking out at dawn in his army boots. It was primarily, I realised, an assertion of will. The effects of running – fitness, clarity of thought, connection with nature – were secondary. They're brilliant and remain a constant throughout my life, but initially running had within it a strong element of two fingers up to the figure who was trying to stop me. It began primarily as a reaction to threat, and in continuing to do it, often in secret, it became in itself a symbol of resistance. I ran in boots. Luckily, it was also something I was fairly good at. My point is: there was ego in there. Fight. Something I had buried in recent years. For this marathon, this challenge, I dug up old coals and threw them on the fire of my burning ambition. Then I stoked them with a punchy, direct and rather childish mantra, which roused the flames and stirred the flickering iridescent furnace of my soul like a red-hot poker.

Fuck her.

I know, it's slightly embarrassing to share.

Fuck her.

But it felt so good to say it. An acceptance of something.

However much I tried to deny it, rationalise it, gain an understanding, see it from her point of view, her actions had hurt me, I had to recognise that. I also had to recognise that deep down I was bothered by the injustice. The sheer relentlessness of it. So then forgive me while I say it one last time.

With respect. *Fuck her.*

In its favour, it's a devastatingly simple and easily understood mantra when blood sugar levels are plummeting. The most important criterion is: it worked. It also had an adaptable quality: I could extrapolate it out to the whole world. according to my mood. With only a minor adaption, it could become fuck him; fuck them; fuck that; indeed, fuck anything and everything that had ever held me back in reality or in the kaleidoscope-like projection loop we're all playing in our heads constantly. The point is, I'd recognised a deep anger that had remained unaddressed.

To say it out loud was to release a shiver of adrenaline and excitement rippling down my spine. It was shockingly new, indecently thrilling and made me want to do many manly things simultaneously: headlock an Alsatian, invade the nearest village, creosote a fence, chop wood, drive a really big lorry, be an extra on the film *Gladiator*, bite the head off the nearest chicken, check the oil in my car, change a light bulb, punch a horse.

This was big, the relief was huge.

I wish you every luck in finding your mantra. It might not be as rude as mine, might be a lot ruder or meditative or upbeat. It just has to be fundamentally true for you. Ring your own bell.

The final piece of the pre-marathon jigsaw slotted into place and with it the moment of enlightenment. I realised exactly what running this marathon was giving me the opportunity to finally do.

21

The juice

At this juncture I'd like to refer you to the main title of this book: *26.2 Miles to Happiness*.

Slightly overblown, I admit, but containing a kernel of truth.

Is it really that simple? you might ask.

What is its great secret? you implore, reaching for the biscuits and putting on the kettle.

Well, I've already presented the case. Obviously there's loads of physical stuff. Running a marathon on any level makes you loads fitter, physically and mentally. The benefits of fitness are unarguable: every day the papers ring with scientific studies attesting to the good news.

But I'm also talking beyond that. There are other reasons. In a chaotic world, it offers order. In an occasionally unjust world, where honest endeavour often crashes on the fickle rocks of reality, it gives you a direct correlation between effort and reward. Indeed, the more you submit to its demands, the more you get; it's a sliding scale of mental and physical transformation. You act yourself into a different person; different habits embed themselves and change you.

On a personal level, where you might feel anonymous, passed over, not valued, the marathon is an event that gives you a day of guaranteed drama with you as the hero.

It's fun and tough in all the right proportions. It's a private drama played out in public, an orgasm of aerobic fun. It allows you to express anger or frustration in a safe environment without having to pay out to punch cushions.

I'm going to go one step further now, so brace yourself.

I also sincerely believe the marathon offers the very real hope of personal redemption, a defeating of personal demons.

The kettle's boiled now, this is a moment that calls for your favourite mug. Lean back, put your feet up. I'm away again, off-piste, skiing haphazardly down the black slope of the human psyche with only the most rudimentary of ski ploughs at my disposal.

(Deep breath.)

It strikes me that most damage occurring to us in life happens at a level beyond words. This might be caused by words or action, but they affect our brains, behaviour and thoughts on a cellular level. Possibly as a result of this, there seems to be a limit to the usefulness of purely talking therapies.

This is not to say therapy isn't useful. I reckon it is, profoundly so: it helps you relate to your life with more awareness; it can help you view yourself, and others, more compassionately. There are skills to be learned, insights gained on the chair with those wonderful people who devote their lives to helping others. I'm all for it. Religion too. Whatever gets you through the long night and helps you face the clear morning. Good luck! It's just, there's an absurdity there too, which is a bit disconcerting. Often, when driving to therapy, I'd be feeling essentially good about my life but trying desperately to dredge up some old memory so that I could get value for money. Maybe it's my upbringing or a Protestant work ethic. In all probability, I'm just tight – but after a while I thought there was a bit of moaning in there, self-pity perhaps. As if I was just returning to the same place on a weekly basis for a good gripe. That's not to discourage anyone from going: pain spreads its wings far and wide, carrying problems infinitely more troublesome and traumatic than my load. It's just that I saw an end to it – and at the end, not much was solved. Because there are moments in life that point out who you are, little episodes, and they told me that despite all the talking I'd done to escape and get over my past, I still carried the memories of violence with me. They'd been encoded, internalised. Triggers remained in my psyche.

Round the house, if I heard quick footsteps upstairs, I'd be transported back from my perfectly safe house in North London to Scarborough, where I was a quivering 13-year-old cowering in the corner as her clogs fired off the kitchen floor. Those sense memories are hard to erase.

At the age of 47, every now and again as I settle into an evening at home, I am flooded with an overwhelming feeling of relief when I realise on a fundamental level I am safe here. It's like a little bugle of victory sounding in my heart and is often accompanied by the urge to go to Oddbins and begin celebrating. This shizzle goes deep, bruv, and no amount of talking can get you through it.

It seemed with the marathon I had stumbled upon a solution.

If the problem was beyond words, then surely, so too was the answer. It had to be something I did, an action.

(Still with me? Grab a biscuit, chocolate hobnob if you're not training. If you are training, maybe a plain digestive or an oatcake.)

People swim the Channel, kayak huge distances, cycle across Europe, climb mountains. In doing so they are receiving something from the experience that helps them. Amid the demands of the exertion, they have found something intrinsic that puts them back together again, however momentarily, in a life that is increasingly fragmented.

Part of the reason I like marathon running is its accessibility. Anyone can do it. No real kit is necessary beyond a decent set of trainers, no travel involved. All the means are literally on your doorstep. Running, that most natural and elemental of activities. The marathon is long enough to be doable by most people, an immense struggle but achievable. It might not have the outdoorsy nature appeal of kayaking or a mountain – which is a drag, because I love nature – but what it does have, especially a big one, is people, lots of people. And people are nature. And I love people.

(Stop choking on your biscuit, this is deep stuff.)

As I ran marathons and came up against the Wall, I began to really wrestle with the question: What did the marathon mean? As I focused down into proper training – being inspired by club mates, considering pain and how to deal with it, matters of mental fortitude – I began to see the Wall not as a force that rendered me powerless but rather as something that I could do battle with. To do this, I knew that I was going to have to get determined, angry even.

This troubled me.

Maybe because I had witnessed and been victim of so much anger growing up, I had gone to great lengths to avoid it as an adult, both my own and others'. When out and about, my senses were and are primed to any suggestion of incident. I see the problem before it happens; my vibe detector is incredibly acute, and I pick up very quickly on changes in atmosphere. This can be very useful. It means I tend to avoid confrontation, but it can also get a bit tiring, and sometimes I might overreact. Some people are freer with their anger, and that's not necessarily a bad thing.

Therapy had unwittingly fed into my anti-anger crusade. I'd spent a lot of time working out how to forgive people – or rather, the person who shall remain nameless. I'd accommodated her behaviour, rationalised it. We are after all, at some level, always doing our best with what we've got. We all come from and are a reaction to events over which we had no control, and I spent a lot of time and energy trying to understand why she might have acted like that. Perhaps in all of this rationalisation I'd never allowed myself to get angry that it had happened in the first place. Even while it was happening, and at an age when I could have resisted, I retreated into myself, acting like I was untouchable, not talking much. It was a form of very silent revenge. I'd become unresponsive as a way of protecting myself and getting through it all, incessant as it was.

As I grew up and my life changed, I carried aspects of this stuff with me. A lot of it was positive. I was and am a pretty chilled-out character. I live and let live, try to understand people, and generally be a force for peace, but in the process I had denied a part of me. In my effort to understand the world, and people in it, I had perhaps closed part of myself off, becoming an unreasonably reasonable man. And underneath it, there was an anger that I had never recognised, which bubbled over in odd places: the car; round the house; on the football pitch. This is not to say I was a psychopath. There was just something in my make-up that wasn't ringing true. Outwardly, I was the uber-chilled, do anything for anybody, Northern bloke around the village – but sometimes, I'd see myself in the mirror and my resting face was a bit scowly. On an afternoon I'd find myself lost in violent fantasy over an innocuous road rage incident that had happened months previously. On social media, I'd find myself having a row with a stranger before I'd even got out of bed on a morning.

These weren't the actions of a man of peace!

Something was gnawing away at me that needed attention. There was, it seemed, a rage within that I'd never given voice to or found an outlet for. On a very simple level I'd never expressed anger at the years living with she who cannot be named and what had happened there. I'd internalised it all – and it came out at traffic lights, imagined threats to my family or at 50/50 challenges at football. (May I take this opportunity to apologise to anyone who's played football with or against me, particularly between the years 2004 and 2010.)

Is it a stretch to say that we live in a fairly angry society? On the roads, on social media, there's a lot of simmering rage about.

Mostly suppressed, but even that effort seems to be resulting in lots of substance problems, antidepressants, boozing and binging.

For me, running helped. As I ran more and faster, I began to see it as a harmless channel for residual and undefined rage from childhood. It could give me permission to fight back and said it was OK to run hard. It also had the advantage that I was only hurting myself; running was self-directed, cleansing even. Football had broken my own wrist and other players' ribs and fingers.

As I examined it and really looked at the marathon, the Wall emerged as a formidable adversary. But like all adversaries, it carried within it the potential for my redemption and self-knowledge. As the marathon approached and the goal of a sub-3 clarified, I began to see the Wall not as a purely physical entity. It became a physical manifestation of the internal voices in my mind. Voices that had stemmed from she who cannot be named.

The Wall became my stepmum, the stepmum became the Wall.

(Final dunking of the biscuit now. Double dunk if you fancy it.)

At the age of 47, I reckoned that maybe it was time finally to fight back. To show myself. Put a flag in the ground and slay this demon once and for all. I had to end this nonsense, put this drama to bed. Battle with the Wall, break through. Defeat it and her.

In order to do this, I knew I had to train hard and remorselessly, eradicate every physical and mental weakness in my make-up.

It was as simple and as beautiful and as easy to understand as that.

Finally, I had found my Why.

The hero must defeat the monster.

PART 3

The Battle: Miles 20–24

Mile 20. Poplar.
We go again

Goal time – 02:16:00. Actual time – 02:16:20. Reset – 00:00:00

I am desperately scanning the roadside up ahead of me for the 20-mile marker. It's a massive part of my special plan. *Where is it? Coming up, surely... there it is! 80 yards up on the left. Good, good.*

Pace is slowing now, not a lot, but fractionally. I can feel it, it's inevitable really, everyone slows. However fit, however mentally determined, we are now in a state of managed atrophy. We factor that in. That's why I was looking to crest the first 13.1 miles in around 88 minutes. This gives me a time cushion of about two minutes in the second half. Not that I want to think too much about the cushion. If you're too aware of the cushion, you start to rest your weary head on it, then you sink into it and all is lost. No, get the cushion, put it in the cupboard, forget it. Still, I'm eating into it now; I reckon each mile is about seven minutes (ish). I'm losing 10 seconds a mile. This is going to go to the wire. Marginal gains, marginal losses, nip and tuck.

Usually, Mile 20 is where I roll up the psychological white flag. The excuses pop out, justifications. By this time, I'm polishing up the phrasing for my perfectly reasonable post-race monologue. *I ran a good race, I gave it my all, etc.*

Today's different, I have a plan. A cunning plan that goes straight to the top of Tonkinson's slightly unorthodox Top Tips, along with urinating on the run and no food before long runs.

A big help in achieving any goal is chunking it down, is it not? We all know this. You don't never drink again, you just don't drink today. You don't change the world, you change yourself. That's not new news.

It's the same deal with the marathon. Twenty-six miles feels too long to race, so there's a need to break it up into component parts in order to get through it. In terms of mental framing, I've heard many methods to make the miles feel more manageable. Some run to Mile 16, then tell themselves they're running a 10-mile race. Some chunk it down into four sections of 10 kilometres each. In York, I'd subdivided the distance into three 10-kilometre chunks followed by two parkruns and finally five laps round the track. This had the advantage that the longer the race went on, the shorter the distances got – easier to run, like a descent. No matter how tired you are, you can always run a parkrun, and after two of those, five laps round the track is no bother. I'd done that in training when knackered so many times. The disadvantage is obvious: it's way too complicated. Even now, after I've had a coffee, it's hard to get my head round: 22 miles into marathon, your head's a mushy mess. Calculations are impossible. No wonder I slowed down in York; I got confused during the second parkrun!

For London I needed a new tactic, a simple, clear technique along with the mantra to liberate my body without disabling my mind.

One was the goal. The three goal idea, although useful for some, hadn't worked for me. One single message was seared into my mind – sub-3. That's it. Nothing more. No get-out clause. No lifeboats. Anything else would represent failure.

I also had the mantra. Great fuel.

In terms of the mechanics of the last 6 miles, the big push, I was being pulled in several different directions as to the best way of looking at it. Lots of wise souls view the marathon as a run to 20 miles followed by a race of 6 miles. This makes perfect sense, but I wanted to refine it a bit further. Six miles felt a bit of a long race when I knew I'd already be close to my limit. Why not, I thought, race to Mile 25? I had stumbled upon the doctrine of *the last mile takes care of itself.*

Why not use it? Race 5 miles. Start again. Use Mile 20 as a launching pad, a platform from which to dive into the chaos of it.

And given that, given that we need a reboot and we're trying to fool the Central Governor, why not go the whole hog and restart the watch? Really start again. And really race. Race as hard as you can to 25. Overtake people in the last stages of the race, be one of those runners for the first time. Because if I hit Mile 25 at speed, there's no way on earth I'm not beating three hours. If it's at all possible, I'm having it from there.

Mile 25, then, became the end. The Central Governor was hoodwinked, bedazzled, conned and furious. Tricked again. (*We had this in Victoria Park!*)

The plan was set.

As I surge towards Mile 20, I chug the last of my drink, quickly gobble the last gel and cast the wrappers aside. It's a relief to be rid of all encumbrances. I've been doing gels every 40 minutes, chomping pastilles every couple of miles, all gone now. The slight strain of unwrapping the gels and the fidgeting with pocket shenanigans had been an increasing pain. To be rid felt symbolic.

Just running now, finally. Pure focus. The Marathon and me. This confrontation. Not even Cova can help me now.

As I pass Mile 20, my legs really hurting, my breath coming in anxious hot gasps, I hit reset on my watch and look down.

00:00:00.

The race starts here to Mile 25. Don't even think that, not 25, because then you'll think about the last 20 miles and how tired you are. No mercy for the Central Governor!

No past, no future. You've just started a 5-mile road race. I look down again.

00:00:04.

Time to push.

22

Super Mario catch-up

Two weeks post-marathon, I turned out as a volunteer at the club track championships. It was a lovely, innocent summer evening, a perfect re-entry into the world of running after two weeks very gently jogging on grass. Recovery was slow, both physically and mentally. Limbs had yet to come back to life after the efforts of the day. London marathon runners walked slowly around the infield, either as timekeepers or giving out drinks to exhausted runners. Victory and defeat had to be dealt with in different ways. Every marathon changes you in ways you cannot necessarily predict; it's an experience that breaks down all defences, siphons off some possibilities and opens up others. As the protective veneer reforms, it is cocooning a slightly different personality.

Runners exchanged war stories at the coffee booth, talking about pace mess-ups, surprises of the day, reflections from the front.

Loitering by the cake stand, I spied Mario. It was the first time I'd seen him since the 5-kilometre mark on the day itself. That morning he'd been a focused hungry shark. In conversation, he's a very gentle, smiley San Franciscan – although he's also an extremely successful Bloomsberg executive, so it's complicated.

He was still buzzing after a personal best of 02:45:26. (Fast!) We talked mental tactics; I was keen to get his secrets from the front of the pack. As we scoffed flapjacks and watched races unfold on the track before us, I ventured that the mental side of things can get a bit ugly in the marathon. 'Oh yeah,' he agreed. 'Absolutely. It has to. It's not a nice thing.' We were both still in the post-marathon bubble. A sharp but serene state of consciousness that perhaps lent an unusually frank nature to the chat.

'How do you do it?' I asked. 'How do you get faster like you do. Push yourself harder?'

'Well,' he sipped his coffee furtively, looking at me with a slightly confessional air, 'I imagine my family is being held hostage and they'll be killed if I don't get there on time. It's actually a fairly detailed scenario but it seems to work.'

He shared this as if it were not one of the most absurd things I'd heard in my adult life, and we moved on to other areas. I let it go with a mental note that I could obviously squeeze it a bit more in the mantra department.

Would that work for me? I wondered. I'd probably get delirious, jog off the course to the nearest phone box and call the police. It might actually make me too angry to run. Everyone's different, aren't they? It's not as if my mantra wasn't absurd: she who cannot be named was long gone. I was hardly going to ring her after the race to tell her the time. It's not as if she'd care if I did. We were constructing and living in a world of symbols. To be fair, I'd seen Mario's wife and kids, who were a delightful bunch.

We gazed out onto the infield. All done now. London and all it meant was slipping into the past. Athletes of all ages and abilities were running in front of us, jumping, throwing javelins. It was like a school sports day reunion. Their energy was teasing us back into running, an open invitation to the summer.

Mario downed his coffee, turned to go back to the clubhouse, but just before leaving he stopped abruptly. 'You know the weirdest thing about it? The day itself?'

'I don't know. What?'

'I loved it, I absolutely loved it and it was intense and I was completely focused on getting a PB.'

'And saving your family.'

'Of course. Of course.' He laughed. He wasn't finished, there was something he'd just thought of, a truth just stumbled upon. 'The strangest thing, about the day, is—' Mario leaned in closer, conspiratorially. 'I can't remember anything about it. Not a second. Especially of the last six miles. It's all blank, a complete haze. Can you?' His eyes were open in a state of utter blank befuddlement. 'Can you remember anything at all?'

Miles 21, 22. Limehouse to Shadwell. Knocked out

Goal time – 07:00/14:00. Actual time – 07:10/14:24

The 5-mile race doesn't last long. Sod that for a game of soldiers. I try, I surge for 200 yards or so, overtake a few, then it's just an effort to maintain any position at all. Has it helped? Hard to say. It feels like a boxer throwing a lazy jab into the air as an opponent pummels his ribs mercilessly. There's no winning this. It's just too hard. Not only that, everyone around me is battling too; I'm in the zone where everybody is trying to beat three hours. They are fit, Tough Mudders. It is blindingly obvious that I will not be overtaking too many people; not that I'm aware of them beyond a sporadic swirl of bodies, vests and shorts. If anything, I'm just desperately trying to stay in this stream; my vision has narrowed.

One way the restarting the watch thing helps is that it helps me understand the time easily. It renders calculations on the move a cinch. I need to run every mile in seven minutes, which means hitting 5 miles bang on the nose of 35 minutes. This is all I have to do. All that training to do this, time to lock into the default setting. All systems are go.

Problem is, I'm not doing it. There's a glitch in the system: I'm running 07:10s. That will eat into the cushion very quickly. Torture. This is torture. My feet sting, my legs a deadweight, my breath is anguished. I'm panicking, starting to unravel, feeling a bit sorry for myself. I feel like I'm being hounded by something, tracked by a malevolent force closing in on me. In a way, it's like I'm scared of something, a nameless entity. The crowd's urgings seem somehow barbaric in their ceaseless demands. It's so loud now, committed, overwhelmingly full throttled in its support, but in my weakened state it feels harsh, I'm a bit defensive.

Not far now! Three and a half miles. Tell you what, you do it.

Looking good. That's a joke, right? You're joking now? Tell me you're joking.

I'm doing my best and I love you all. I am. I'm just not in a good place right now. I want to lie down or fall into a hot bath for an hour. Sink into a sack of amniotic fluid and be a foetus again. This life is too much for me.

Is the mantra helping? Hard to say. Have I thought of it, of her? Yes, at times. Am I thinking of it now? Not really. It's just one voice among the multitude in my head.

The problem with the mantra is it makes me think of the bad old days; this is not good, though the reason I chose it remains valid. The bullishness surfaces amid the rabble. It's double-edged. What is designed to give me ultimate strength is also the source of my greatest weakness. The will is still strong, I'm in this fight. I want to win it, but every step's a world in itself containing within it an open-ended and very tempting option to slow down on the next one. I've lost momentum. The watch reads 00:16:47. I'm confused and alone, somewhere past Mile 22. Less than 3 miles to go to reach Mile 25. *Push this. Fucking go. Hit this.* There's no give in me, I will not let this go for a second. The 5-mile thing is a non-starter, too long. It's a race to the next lamppost, a tree by the side of the road. Zatopek again; Emil, you legend. *Feel bad. Run faster.* George Eden. Dear George. With his glasses steaming up, running through the fields. Rudy, Ra. Do it so you can walk down The Mall and see them after the race and give him something to be proud about. Dig in. Tony Audenshaw; he missed it by six seconds that year. Do this now or never. *Enjoy yourself.* Scrap! Scrap!

But I'm slowing. Despite all this, slightly slowing, despite all efforts. Is it the Central Governor's revenge?

Then, it couldn't be more perfect. There's a slight weakening on a stride, for the first time today a break in the pattern of movement forward, a stutter in the machine that leaves me back on my heels a touch, not stopping but hesitating – at that very second, I become aware of a small but significant gathering of runners off to my left, containing within it a mass of dark energy. I can't believe it, hadn't even contemplated it within the realms of possibilities. But there it is, crushingly unreal but undeniably clear as day, bobbing in the air above us all.

It's the sub-3 pacer sign, gliding in alongside me, like a black shark's fin. The grim reaper.

And holding the sign is the sub-3 pacer. A perfectly normal-looking but extremely fit guy in his knee-length compression socks, pitter-pattering away on the tarmac, still holding perfect form. A small group of runners are latched on to his coat-tails, sporting thousand-yard stares. It's a plucky platoon of even pacers. They've made the right call. I went alone and I've been picked off. Rookie's error. I've done this before.

They match strides with me for a second and then slowly, inevitably pass and move off into the distance, along with any chance of a sub-3 marathon.

I try, I really do. With every sinew, I attempt to go with them. Part of the problem is it feels like I've been punched in the face. I had not envisioned this, and I'm not ready for it. I'd deliberately set off at a slightly faster pace than the pacers, I wanted to write my own story, run my own race. With the training I'd done, the positive talk scaffolding I'd set up around the event, I had not thought of this scenario. I didn't want to see the pacers, never mind be overtaken by them.

For a second, I can't believe it. I feel hollowed out, filleted.

Again. It's happening again. After all this effort, it's won. *She's* won. The whole thing. I won't come back from this.

That's it, then. Fair enough. Did my best. What was I thinking?

My head has gone completely. It's on me, all on me. Failure. I'm sinking into it. It is a familiar, smothering, darkly comforting sensation. This is old news. I can do this as well.

23

Black Tuesday, 7 p.m. Three weeks before the marathon

I am on a table and a man is prodding my right foot repeatedly. He's being very aggressive and seems to possess a forensic knowledge of where exactly to apply pressure for maximum pain. It's like he doesn't realise the foot is attached to me and that it is sending messages to my brain. When will it end, this merciless scrunching, bending, slapping? A whimper is forming in the back of my throat, which I struggle to suppress. It's the quiet insistency of it all that disturbs me. The complete silence, the non-recognition of the discomfort that I am doing so well to contain. Nobody's saying anything. I'm reverting to childhood. I need a reward of some kind, a sweet perhaps. At the very least, somebody needs to call me a brave little soldier very quickly.

Don't worry, we have not jumped into a hostage situation, I've paid for this. It's massage, Chinese method – Tui na. Serious stuff. And it's hurting, seriously killing me. Acute pain nibbling at my consciousness. I'm no good with real pain. I can do the long-haul stuff, the self-inflicted marathon experiment; I'm getting increasingly good at that. But I remain fragile. Sometimes a sound can hurt me, if I get too handsy with the gear stick on the wife's Seat and that metallic shrill grate kicks in. I whinny and jump like I'm on a fairground rodeo. Stoicism is not my strong point. I'd never get a tattoo or piercing for that reason; why choose it? I move away from jarring pain and danger. That's why I like the marathon. Any pain is self-inflicted and it's not really dangerous, is it? The only danger is injury. Training can leave you perilously close to overload that tips over into an injury that threatens the race itself.

Which is where we are. Project Sub-3 under attack.

The man's name is Andrew; he is a kind, intelligent man who has devoted his life to the workings of the feet and lower legs, the intricacies of the pressure points and bones contained within this spaghetti junction of stress and imbalance. His sessions are, to quote Claire, 'hardcore, tear-inducing nightmares' and 20 minutes in I can testify to that. A tear is indeed developing in the corner of my eye. I will not release it. Instead, I breathe as he digs deep into the accumulated gristle on my foot, caused by all that bad running form.

An hour earlier, he had seen my foot for the first time. 'Ah yes,' he said, 'Morton's toe.'

It was as if he were greeting an old friend. My second toe was longer than my big toe, apparently. Well, there's no arguing with it, it is. This affects the way weight transfers into my foot, and the way I transfer weight into the foot is also affected by the fact that my feet seem to be very flat by nature. Problems.

Andrew made a few exploratory forays into the area round the back of my foot with his nimble fingers. A little probe here, light pressure there. This was accompanied by gentle sighs and half giggles of recognition. He then stood up and spilled out his diagnosis like an urgent declaration of love. 'The tendon is fusing with the bone, the arches have collapsed. This has resulted in numerous micro tears. Not only loads of scar tissue, but also a lot of dead, what we call zombie, tissue.'

Now, I love zombies as much as the next film fan, but any connection between zombies and my foot sounded a bit chilling. 'So, my foot,' I managed to respond, 'is dying?'

He seemed very excited and rapped on the side of my foot, like you might check a wall. 'In some places it's already dead. Now,' he grinned, looking up like Doc Brown in *Back to the Future*, 'we must bring it back to life '

The diagnosis made total sense. From time to time the foot had felt, in places, inert, completely lacking in sensitivity. A weight of flesh and bone to be carried around as opposed to a sensitive instrument to run on.

So we're left with all this palaver. The crunching and nipping and kneading and knocking; it's a resuscitation job, except it's not mouth to mouth, it's hand to foot. I'm urging him on, sort of; I'll do anything to run again. To get off the table and run properly. I have to run the marathon. I've lost two days already to this. *Aagh.* A noise escapes me, involuntary.

Andrew smiles. This is a good sign, apparently; proceedings come to a halt. He stands up quite jauntily, sweating heavily. This is tough for him as well. Maybe it's time for a rest or a sip of water. A joke perhaps? No.

Reaching under the table, he unearths a black leather bag and plonks it on the table before uttering one of the most frightening sentences I've ever had uttered to me (outside of phone correspondence with the Inland Revenue).

'I'm going to need some implements,' he intoned, 'so we can go deeper.'

Running as much as you do to train for a marathon can put enormous strains on the body. It's a bloody long way. Look at a map, and find a place 26 miles away. You're training your body to run there. When I'm in London, I always think that the marathon is basically running to Watford. Why would anyone want to do that? (This is not a judgement on the good people of Watford or indeed Watford itself. I've had some great gigs there in the past. Well, one great gig ... and it wasn't in Watford.)

So, injury from time to time is no surprise. Trick is, nip it in the bud early. Problem is, most runners aren't like that. We tend towards the bullheaded. Over time we learn to accept certain levels of discomfort. *As long as you can run*, the saying goes, *you're OK*. Most runners of any experience have things that are, on the face of it, wrong with them. They live and train with it. Little strains, muscle problems. They don't give it too much respect. Running and racing is the important thing. Long-term health comes later.

To the outsider, some behaviours may seem hard to understand, excessive even. I am reminded of ultramarathoner Scott Jurek, a gentle vegan soul who, on the eve of a rigorous ultra, tore the ligaments surrounding his left ankle. Did he withdraw from the race the following day? Did he hell! He smothered the ankle in turmeric (?), wrapped it up with gaffer tape and then ran and won a 100-mile race. That's vegans for you. A good friend of mine recently ran the New York marathon while suffering from norovirus. Probably best give him a wide berth – and do not share his water bottle!

I present these tales not as examples of behaviour to aspire to, just as examples of where you can end up. I suppose I'm looking for a reason to explain how I ended up where I ended up, paying a very nice man to lay me down and hurt me for an hour.

The foot had been playing up for a while. I'd had a weird growth on it for six months or so, a ganglion. It was like a very small mountain ridge on the right-hand side of my right foot, a maggot-like swelling under the skin. Pudgy to touch but with a solid mass to it, painless and strange. As far as I could work out, it was tissue that had broken forth within the foot, an eruption of something certainly, an obvious malfunction. It was a potential cause for concern, but it didn't really hurt. That's the thing: I felt its existence but it wasn't problematic. I'm not saying I liked it, but it didn't bother me, and I began to be curious about its ways. The ganglion moved around a bit on my foot within a fairly narrow parameter. This probably sounds weird; I suppose you can get used to anything. Word on the street was that you could get rid of a ganglion by getting a priest to bash it viciously with a King

James Bible, but I didn't have the bottle for that, so I ignored it and continued running. I trussed that foot up tight with my laces and took to the forest; you know the drill.

One morning, miraculously, the ganglion was no longer there. Job done, Dr Tonkinson!

So I proceeded on my merry way, occasionally feeling numb in that area, a numbness that affected my form on that side, a minor but continuous adjustment to my foot placement. Fitness was improving, momentum had been established, and I didn't want to hex anything. The day after the Bath half marathon, the toe on my right foot, the one next to the big toe, really hurt as I walked down the stairs at home. A pins and needles sensation. Very odd. I ignored it and ran on. Can you see a theme developing? Three weeks later, a distinct and sharp ache on my right foot left me limping the last 2 miles of a midweek 10-miler. This was serious. It had crossed a line and was now affecting the run. Ignoring it was impossible. That night I plunged into an orgy of self-diagnosis and depression.

Was it my metatarsal? Had I broken something? That would mean five to six weeks out. What would I do? (We didn't have any turmeric.) I walked the house with a sullen angry face that nobody noticed.

Advice varied. Ice. Peas. Elevation. YouTube offered numerous methods of self-manipulation, which I did long into the night, inexpertly harassing and rubbing my foot under the supervision of internet quacks and self-styled professionals. It was an imprecise science that had little effect on the pain or the limp. At breakfast I was a distant, moody Dad. The darkness of my mood surprised me. The possibility of the marathon being off was, I knew, about to send me spiralling downwards.

I reached out to Claire, she of the cresting testicle, who gave me a number that led me to this room, this table, this horrendous hour, this black leather bag and this Andrew turning to me with a length of what looked like an ivory shoe horn.

'This'll do it.'

He set to work, my hands gripping the side of the table for ballast. By the end of the session I was a gooey puddle of relaxed and battered flesh. The foot, Andrew pronounced, much to my relief and gratitude, was coming back to life. I'd need more hours with him, two or three. I also needed to buy a golf ball and use it to massage pressure points, smother the foot vigorously with Tiger Balm and stretch it. Above all, I needed to rest the foot. Swim but no contact, ease off on the running.

'The thing is,' I impressed upon him, 'I cannot do that. That's the one thing I cannot do.' My voice invited no rebuttal. 'I need another high mileage week, two weeks' taper then an all-out marathon out of this foot.'

'I advise rest,' he countered matter-of-factly.

'But, would it hold? If it had to,' I pressed. 'If I massaged it and golf balled it and drenched it in Tiger Balm, am I damaging myself long term? Can I do this?'

Andrew looked at me in resignation. And then he sighed the sigh of the healer who has been ignored, and his sigh soared into heaven or that other space where the new age types hang out – you know, the crystal merchants and the reiki mob. He'd met people like me before. Driven, haunted souls. Not interested in healing, only the continuation of the path that had hurt them in the first place. 'Looks like we're going to find out.'

Mile 23½. Approaching the Embankment. A bearded intervention

Now brace yourself. Not for the first time I'm going to drop something on you, and it's up to you how you're going to take it.

Right from the off, I'm going to say that I don't believe in angels.

There, I've said it. Although a quick google shows that approximately 40 per cent of the population do, so I won't be too sniffy about the concept. I like to see myself as a rational agent co-existing with other rational agents, muddling through with the information at hand, making mistakes, sometimes getting things right, and all the time operating under the behest of chance elements and happenstance. Neither do I believe in predetermination. I'm a free will advocate. That's one of the attractions of the whole running thing: we create our time through training, preparation, choices we make during the race, etc.

Having said that, I have to admit there have been moments in life when certain individuals have appeared to me *just* when I needed them to send me a message that the decision I was about to make would be disastrous. They've just popped up and then popped off again into the ether. Now this might be hindsight bias, it might be nonsense. After all, loads of people are constantly popping up and off, and we are free to interpret their words and actions however we want to. This doesn't mean they are angelic; it's simply a matter of coincidence! Although, truth be told, it's quite nice to see ourselves as being led or protected by celestial beings in human form and it's definitely possible to feel that some people have 'saved' you in one form or other. On my mobile, my wife is listed as Angel, and I named my elder son after George Bailey from *It's A Wonderful Life*, so draw your own conclusions.

All I'm saying is this: when I absolutely needed someone, something or somebody to give me a boost during the London marathon, when I was at the end of my tether, adrift in the ocean of self-pity and drowning in a primal, elemental psychic sludge, someone just popped up, and then off again.

Maybe it's just that Goethe quote coming back – that one about boldness and magic, the nature of commitment. 'The moment one definitely commits oneself, then Providence moves too. All sorts of things occur to help one that would never otherwise have occurred.'

Picture the scene. I'm 23½ miles in. I've committed. I've done all the training, I've eaten the right food, been to the Mayr and run hungry like the wolf in the mountains. I've eaten a gluten-free Jaffa Cake, smashed my foot till it started working again, even forged a mantra and imprinted in onto my soul. I've reframed this day as a titanic struggle between good and evil, and placed upon it the weight of my very salvation. Now all is lost, the monster has me in its grasp. I am losing, in every second, every faltering step, watching helplessly as the sub-3 pacer runs away in the distance along with my dreams of glory and redemption.

I'm still fighting, but only just. There's a flicker of resistance in each stride as I struggle to maintain pace. Overall, though, the theme is one of unreality. Displacement. I'm being framed by a universe I haven't conceived. I'm behind the sub-3 pacer guy with the sign. I try to shake my stride pattern, and slap my legs in frustration. Nothing doing. Desperately I scan the crowd for a familiar face, begging for a lifeline. It's the stage of the race where more organised types arrange for family and friends to stand, that bit just before the Embankment, the start of the end. The noise is deafening but discordant. It feels like it's being directed at individuals, but maybe that's my mind playing tricks. There's nobody singing for me, that's for sure.

Then, out of nowhere, a bearded man has raised himself up on the roadside steel fence. He's in his mid-30s, I guess, and in jeans and a plain white shirt, he leans forward, pointing at me directly, his eyes ablaze, his voice clear as a bell:

'Paul Tonkinson, you can do this! You're looking good and it's not far. You've got this!'

All I can say is, at that moment it was exactly what I needed to hear, pricking, as it did, the bubble of self-pity that had been inflating around my person.

An angel? Who knows? Was it Providence moving for me? Almost certainly.

What I do know is, to this day I have no idea who this man was.

If you are the man in question, please get in touch, I owe you a drink. No proof necessary, I remember the face. If you're an angel, don't bother, I've heard you don't drink. But you're definitely in line for some wings and I'll ring a till when I get the chance.

What I'm absolutely sure about is this: his certainty and generosity of spirit catapulted me into a different state of mind.

It made me pick my head up and look down the road for the first time in half a mile or so, and what I remember, clear as day, is that when I did the sub-3 pacer was there up the road, his sign bobbing away.

Not only that, but thrillingly, incredibly, at that second, he didn't seem that far away, or rather he wasn't getting further away. There was still a connection, an invisible thread between us. I had contact, however slim.

It's a magical concept, the idea of contact when running. You know when you've got it, you know when you've lost it. There can be a runner just 2 yards in front of you but you feel you have lost contact; or you can be 50 yards behind and confident of catching them up. It's closely linked with will, momentum.

At this stage of the race, as we made our way towards the Embankment, the sub-3 pacer was maybe 80 yards in front of me – but I felt contact, a distant spark that held us together.

Maybe I could do this. Maybe, just maybe, I had got this.

My stride quickened.

As a kid at home, there were times when the activity round the house reached such a spiking pitch that I'd take refuge in the cupboard under the stairs for a moment. It was warm and cosily close in there, with the snorkel parkas, heavy garden coats and the odd Harrington jacket hanging from the wall. Shoes perched on the four-tiered plastic rack, tins of paint languished abandoned on the shelf next to neighbouring never-to-be-used boxes of buttons, redundant and outdated sheaves of household admin. Out of sight and for a brief moment out of mind.

I remember standing there one evening, shaking a bit, gathering my breath before going back outside and over the top again. I was scared, alone, exhausted. This must have been when I was about 14, but the recollection is insistent and clear.

Suddenly, out of nowhere, I felt a still calm voice inside of me saying simply: *This will end, you know. Life will not always be like this. There'll come a time when you'll have a family yourself and look back at this from a distance. It will be over.*

The thought was startlingly obvious, but one I'd never had up to that point.

You can get through this. It's not for ever.

The voice welled up and washed over me, an immense comfort.

You could say it was a spiritual thing, if you're of that inclination. You can suggest it was God reaching out to me. Suffice to say it was accompanied by a deep and profound feeling of absolute relief.

It seems a bit daft to confess that I'd never had this thought before but it's true. She who cannot be named had arrived in my life fairly suddenly. I'd had no control over any of it or anything for years, and had been locked into the daily battle to maintain dignity and survival. Why hadn't I realised this sooner?

Yes. It wouldn't always be like this. I'd grow up and leave this place. Create my own family. And when I did, I could put this right. This was my life *now*, it wasn't my life. There'd come a time when she wouldn't be there. This was a revelation that appeared fully formed in my mind and left me dizzyingly happy.

Life was immeasurably better after that very private moment. Although familiar patterns continued for the next year or so, these had less effect on me. The news had awakened an optimism deep inside of me.

I'd had a glimpse of the future. Like the marathon, the end wasn't very far away.

24

Two weeks before the marathon. Owning Richard

My wife's birthday had morphed into a festival straddling several months (as opposed to the more conventional time and location of one day, one place). Numerous dinners, get-togethers and weekends away had climaxed in *a final*, good old-fashioned disco in a village hall in, of all places, Croyde in Devon. It's testament to my wife's and Croyde's popularity that many of the partygoers from London before Christmas had reconvened in Croyde the following spring to dance to old school tunes, sing a bit of karaoke and generally tie the knot off of the big five-o.

Children gave the evening a more innocent atmosphere than the pre-Christmas bacchanalian orgy. But still, a van selling fish and chips had been arranged to mop up the booze around 10-ish and this had given the hardy drinkers a healthy foundation on which to pour more booze. London spilled out into the quiet Croyde night in a flock of fags and chatter.

'How's it going, Mo?'

Richard's voice pierced the air between us. I'd hardly seen him since Dirty Burger, there'd been little point. I'd gone full marathon monastic, he'd been working and earning with his usual level of commitment and had taken to calling me Mo (Farah) as a joke.

By this stage I was two weeks away from the race. It was all I could think about and I was barely able to conduct a normal conversation without steering it into pace projection analysis. I was a barely functioning marathon lunatic. Fitter than I'd ever been in my life, I had my mantra and a series of bizarre stretches to ease the problems relating to Morton's toe.

'Alright, mate,' I responded. 'I can't and won't complain.'

'We mustn't.' He grabbed me affectionately on the upper arm. 'We must never complain, or explain.'

'Never.'

'You've had some chips.'

'I've had some chips. In fact, I'm having some chips. Good carbs.'

My last longish run of 16 miles had been comfortably dispatched that very afternoon. I'd done the last 4 miles at sub-3 marathon pace with ease. Chips were in order and, why not, mushy peas.

'No booze?'

'No booze.'

We seemed to be in a conversational pattern that resolved around the sharing of basic dietary facts.

'Standing?'

'Yes. Still standing. Like Elton John, outside a chip shop in the open air at—' I checked my watch '—10.55. These facts we know to be self-evident.'

'Have you worked out the meaning of marathon life yet?'

'You'll be pleased to know very nearly. Close to a sign-off on that one.'

'Completed your thesis on the nature of pain and the advantages of it?'

'It's all process, of course, but I have some thoughts.'

'Please hold forth as I light my cigarette without blowing it in your direction.'

In the natural break I continued tucking into my chips, nice and hot, salty carb swords. I felt them going straight to my legs to feed the soft ache left from the afternoon.

'I can't help wondering if the way you're eating those chips is indicative of some pain that you are on the run from?'

Ah. The old pain gambit. I'd thought a lot about pain recently. And it's true, I was scraping out the last few chips rather urgently. But really I was marking time, lulling him in as a thought, an idea that had been crystallising in my head, gathered shape. It was the old Ali rope-a-dope and I was on the cusp of a Croyde chippie rhapsody. 'Pain and its manifestations are everywhere. The chips, the fags, booze, running. Everywhere the interplay between pain and pleasure. Satisfaction, alienation. It's a heady mix. We can't escape it.'

'We can't,' he echoed ironically. 'It's inevitable.'

'We agree on that, then. It is inevitable.'

'And yet. And yet.' No more chips left now. I was folding the paper up; a ball was forming, hardening within my grip. 'It seems to me that as we push into it, if we do, if we take our time to question it, understand its source, then we can see it, not as something to be the victim of but as a challenge to be accepted. Then we can battle it with our will, thrust ourselves into it wholeheartedly without reservation, even welcome it. And then,' I said, holding the paper in my hand as I did so, wondering whether to risk throwing it into the open bin two metres to my right. 'And then—' Maybe I would chance it. If I was on my own, I'd do it no bother. If I went for it and missed, that would weaken my point. '—if we do that, if we really take it on without fear, open-hearted, giving it everything—' I released the paper with a deft flick of the wrist. And with a graceful arc, the paper sailed into the bin. '—we can transform it.'

PART 4
Tipping Point

Mile 24. Blackfriars. The magical possibility

From somewhere, renewal.

I don't know whether it's the beardy bloke shouting who has jolted me back to life, or the training kicking in, or a delayed effect from all the gels I've scoffed, but as I make the descent down to the Embankment my vision has cleared. Perhaps it's simply proximity to the finish. I'm starting to feel its pull now: 2 miles, that's 8 laps of a track. I can do that. Time's tight but... possible. This is still on. For the first time since Mile 18 and the Wall, I'm feeling hopeful. The terrible probability that I wouldn't beat three hours has passed over into the magical possibility that I might. My form is back. I'm running a bit taller, the fast light steps have returned. Cova is on my shoulder.

Momentum is mine. Feelings of depression have been replaced by an all-consuming but positive anxiety. I've noticed this when close to anything really important; having kids comes to mind. The closer you get to the moment of birth, the more unlikely the whole thing becomes. It's so big and the build-up is so tense and vivid and real that, by the time it happens, it seems unbelievable.

Sub-3's like that. I'm literally in the running for it, close, stupidly close. But it's eluding me. It's like running in a vacuum. My head can't do sums anymore and the whole *reset your watch* thing seems like the actions of a lunatic undertaken several months ago, so much has changed since then. It seemed like a good plan, but all it means at this moment is that the digits on my watch don't relate to anything. I've got, I reckon about 20 seconds to make up in the next two miles or so. There'll be no coronation in the last mile. I'd been dreaming of a scenario whereby I could enjoy the last stretch. Ha! What a joke! What arrogance! All the months of training, the no drinking, no eating before long runs, the miles and miles for this. This is a desperate dash, a rescue job. The only good news is that my head's back, I'm in the fight again. I'd disappeared there for a mile or so.

And then I run under Blackfriars Bridge.

In the semi-darkness I can see the crowds in the light on the other side; they are cheering loudly, their voices swamped by a huge sound system that's playing massive throbbing house music. I'm getting rave flashbacks now, my body suddenly flooding with endorphins. Everybody's feeling it. Collective pace quickens. We are running into the crowds, the noise that greets us. The knowledge that we are getting close to the finish now, the crowds, the music, it seems to propel us through the fatigue. Suddenly it all feels very tribal, we are shouting at each other, urging each other on. *Come on! Come on!* My head is shredded by the beats, we have lost leave of our senses. As we come into the light, the noise from the crowd is a full-throated roar. They are giving and demanding every effort. I love them. There's nothing between us at all in this second. I'm happy – fuck me, I'm happy. It's an angry joy, and I'm some kind of fool for wanting it, but I'm so, so pleased to be here, straining everything, thrashing myself.

I've come back to life. For the first time since going under at the 18 mile mark, I feel fully conscious. It's hope that's done this. I'm full of it.

Could I do it?

Could this be the day?

Could I walk down The Mall after the race and see little Rudy and Ra with all this finally done and dusted, this twisted quest over?

The sub-3 pacer is, if anything, getting closer and ... who's that? Running 30 yards ahead of me on the side of the road? Dominic.

I'd completely forgotten about him. Dominic in the club vest, his head starting to roll a bit. It's Tuesday on the track again, I'm used to following him, but this time I'm catching him with every stride. My legs have gone up a gear, I'm motoring.

When I pull up next to him, I can see he's gone. The usual graceful style has disintegrated into separate parts. I want to take him with me, drag him out of his fugue. I want to be his bearded bloke.

'Come on! Let's go. You can do this!!'

I'm in his face.

'Short steps. Let's go.'

I'm not really making sense and he looks way too gone to change anything. He doesn't do short steps, he does long languorous strides; that's why I can never catch him on the short stuff, maybe it's a mechanical thing. Titchy Tonk with his tiny steps. Whatever it is, he's not coming with me. I want to drag him along, but no dice. Without speaking, he waves me on blankly. After a final look, I leave him.

PART 5

Better

25

Mile 25. The final corner

I ask a fellow runner for the time. The proper time. The accumulated time since the start of this business.

02:52:15.

I try to do the sums: 7 minutes and 45 seconds for the last mile and 365 yards. Tight. This is tight. I'm scared. it's an urgent, delirious panic. I can't believe I'm so close and I can't believe I'm going to do it. I think of Tony Audenshaw and his 3 hours – and 6 seconds. I think of Dominic and his 3 hours – and 24 seconds. How do you come back from that? I don't know whether I could. But this is doable. Now. If I speed up just a little. Fractions, that's all it is. My muscles are tightening now, there's a suggestion of cramp in my right calf. I've never had it before. Surely not? I change my style a bit, swinging from the hips a bit more. The finish is a bit twisty and turny; bizarrely, there's fewer people now. The crowds thin out here, they're all on The Mall and The Mall is... where? Where's The Mall?

The finish is messing with me. This mile is lasting forever. I'm passing people though, cutting through. I'm one of those people finally, finishing strong.

I can see him, there's no doubt now, I'm catching him. Yes. Yes. The sub-3 pacer is passed, suddenly shrunken and human after his supernatural appearance at 22.5 miles. He's just a guy who's trying to help people after all, and he's alone now, which means they've all left him. The sign looks vaguely comic now, emptied of all power. They've piggybacked on him for Miles 25 and 26 and then they hop off for the big finish. Either that, or he's slowing down. Am I in it? Am in the sub-3 zone? There are marshals with hi-vis vests and they're messing with the cordons. And am I? Am I on the right side? Yes. I am. *Leg it. Fuckin' leg it.*

I don't think I've run with such fear since the time I sprinted away from the store detectives when they caught me nicking the complete works of Samuel Beckett in Waterstones Manchester, March 1988.

It's a bizarre fact that the only mile marker in the London marathon without a big clock next to it telling you how long you've been running is the marker for 26 miles. The reasons for this may be practical; perhaps the organisers reason that you are so close to the finish you'll find out soon enough anyway. Me, I think it's a decision designed to ramp the nerves up to such an extent that you can barely breathe. Of course, normal runners can just look at their watch; they didn't restart their watch at Mile 20. Fucking idiot features here did, so I'm lost. I know we're close, but ... nothing's certain. Anything can happen. Every runner is a solitary unit lost in a frenzied dash to the finish – whose power is irresistible. We are hypnotised.

Another corner, how many more corners? This is it, yup, the last one. I've been here before. Visualised this moment a thousand times. Get round this corner. Look to the clock. If it says 02:59:00 ... sprint. Get your head down and leather it. It's the putting green on the south cliffs again in your bare feet on a morning. How many times in your life have you sprinted? Hundreds of times, you've dragged one up from nowhere. Sprint, then. Sprint. Sprint like your life depends on it.

Just get round this corner.

There's an old bloke very close to me as we approach. We're both trying to cut across at its sharpest angle, but we don't want to collide. He's wearing an all black kit, looks at least 15 years older than me with his head down and he's not really paying attention.

It seems inevitable we're going to go arse over tit. Which way's he going? Make a decision!! We almost catch each other; for a microsecond I slow down and urgently usher him through. I can't believe it, I'm going to miss it cos of this old bloke.

Go on! Go on!!

He's through and out and round the corner and then I am just behind him. We erupt into The Mall. It's immediately much lighter and we are hit by a wall of noise from the crowd. A frenzied high-pitched collective scream of encouragement as we spill out. I step to the left straight away, look up, towards the Palace, home and the finish – and there, not 80 yards in front of me, closer than I remember, is the clock. And on the clock the numbers tell me I've been running for 2 hours and 59 minutes and something.

I sprint.

26

Finished

The finish down The Mall is shorter than I remembered. Not a long torturous surge, more of a quick dash. I put my head down and go. My breath's an urgent, continuous gasp, I'm driving into every stride, pumping my arms as much as possible. It's a very mechanical response to being on the verge of what I've been after for half my adult life.

With 30 yards to go, I look up.

02:59:15 ... 02:59:16.

I know I've done it then. I could walk it from here.

It's in. Job done. Job fuckin' done. Yes. Fuckin' yes. I clench my fists, swearing with joy, and realise that I am in a bubble of runners, men and women of about the same age doing exactly the same thing. We've done it. We've all done it.

I cross the line.

02:59:21.

What a result. What joy to stop. Finally stop. Get in. Get the fuck in. (I won't relay all the swearing, there was a lot of it.) I'm awash with relief, totally giddy. Shaking hands. Everyone's swearing, punching fists and looking at watches in the immediate vicinity. People are hugging. Then it's getting busy at the finish and increasingly desperate, some are just sneaking under the 3. Some are missing it. I'm being ushered up the finishing funnel on my suddenly useless legs.

It's over, all of it. I can't believe it.

Over.

And I'll have done it forever. The next few days I'll feel it echoing in my legs as I walk up and down stairs, the marathon singing in my limbs. For the rest of my life I'll have done it – and if you run one, if you look at it and focus, create a mantra and really go for it on the level you want to, you will have done it too.

Write your story. Find your why. Win your race. Carry it with you. Brilliant.

Now, ideally, I'd soak up the atmosphere at the mass finish after the race and chat to all and sundry, but because of my 'celebrity' status I'm ushered to a special area a few hundred yards from the finish for a massage and possible press interviews. What this means in practice is that the poor liaison girl gets both barrels of my post-race euphoria babbling high as I unpack the entire contents of what will turn out to be this book to her in under two minutes in a stream of consciousness.

It's like I've awoken from a 30-year sleep and she's the first person I'm speaking to.

We go into some gardens that have been reconfigured as an all-purpose media and recovery zone for world-class athletes, high-ranking celebrities and Northern chancers.

With some relief she palms me off to the massage table and I sip water and relax as my legs are gently stroked. There's no post-York fruit to the nose this time round. In fact, the masseur says that my legs are in pretty good shape. If anything, he says, I could have gone faster. Then it's out to the long and rigorous round of press interviews, none at all, and I'm spat out into the world, the whole process having taken only 20 minutes.

I'm tired, but it's the cleanest tired in the world. It's the tiredness of a summer's evening in childhood, running home absolutely famished after a day's footy on the beach, the sweat turning to salt on your neck as you run and kick the ball against the wall again and again. I'll be in this bubble to a greater or lesser extent all week.

But 20 minutes in, I'm floating around like a slightly dehydrated Jesus, there is absolutely no distance between me and the rest of humanity. We are one. I'm helping people with bags, chatting to everyone about their time, giving directions, thanking volunteers. It's loud, and London at its absolute best. Some people recognise me from the running community. We swap times, tell stories. Some know I've been after three hours for years, so it's nice to tell them. The feeling is one of total relief. A huge inner softening. Swelling relaxation.

I'm chatting to everyone. Open. To be grandiose, not for the first time, I am suffused with a deep and overwhelming peace, a resounding and ultimate inner Yes. My work here is done. I have run to the end of running. It has nothing more to ask of me and there's nothing more I can give. I am as beyond stress and anger and misdirected anxiety as it is possible to be. Compassion spreads in all directions to everyone I've ever met or will meet.

Everyone.

She didn't mean any harm.

Let's face it; I couldn't have done it without her. It wasn't all bad anyway. A brilliant cook, her spaghetti bolognese has never been bettered and her rock cakes were to die for. She'd take me out on her motorbike up on Oliver's Mount. How exciting it was to hold on to her as she whizzed round corners; how dangerous and new and different she was to other mums, exotic in her way, a leather-clad Boadicea, cranking up the volume on Diana Ross records on her days off, just a lass from Whitby making her way in life who'd taken the wrong turn. I remember her crying hot tears on her 30th birthday on being so old. She made me tough in ways I wouldn't have been without her – and God knows what her childhood was like. What merry hell was she repeating?

She who cannot be named won't read this, but if she does, if she sees the name and picks it up and is reading it at this very moment, I'd like to say:

It's over now. All over.

I wish you every happiness.

Whatever this is, has ended. I've drawn a line in the sand. Whatever I wanted out of it, I've got. Undeniably.

I don't know if I'll ever want to train for something as hard as this again.

Then I'm on the phone to Ra and Rudy. It's the last picture of the day that I've painted in my head pre-race. I wanted so much to do this, to beat three hours and come back down The Mall and find them here, amid all the thousands of runners chilling out post-race.

There's a bit of tension as I scour the faces in the crowd, looking for them. I have been informed that they are standing by a tree. Which is good to know in a sea of trees. I'm not too worried, though; I'll see them sooner or later. It's extremely pleasant to be wandering here with all the runners, finally at rest, our races run. Some are lying on the grass, some stretching or chomping from the goodie bags. It is, all told, a heavenly scene I'm drifting through – gingerly, on stiffening legs.

How lucky we are to get to do all this. To be fit and run and see our family and go home and sit on the sofa with the dogs and yes, tonight, possibly some wine is called for.

After all, I want to toast this. I want to toast the world. (I also want some toast.)

It's the simplest things in life, this life we lead.

Enjoy yourself!

And then I see them, peeking out from behind a tree, my wife and youngest son, dear Rudy, walking towards me.

26.2. Bonita

Two months after the marathon, I'm on my way into Crouch End for an all too rare shopping trip with my daughter. Her eyes are almost rolling back into her head with excitement as she lists the essential items of the day that we must buy: some nail varnish, hair clips, new tights, the honey that she likes, eggs, sweetcorn. We've come to a set of traffic lights and pause as the village stretches out below us. The post-marathon bubble of serenity has been on a slow puncture for weeks; it's a dear, clear memory, but today I'm stressed out. Money's tight. I could do without this mini spree. I need to be writing and I've got a four-hour round trip later today, to Nottingham.

She jauntily stands beside me, frantically thinking of other stuff she can persuade me to buy in this *I've got Dad where I want him* window.

'Purdey's? We also need Maryland cookies and ... cheese!'

I haven't really talked about Bonita (named after the Madonna song, Spanish for *beautiful*, though my dad maintains to this day the literal Spanish translation is 'skipjack tuna or tinned fish'). She's a fascinating character. Sixteen years old, bright, determined but also highly irritable, prone to the odd hissy fit. There are moments when we bond magnificently; she's very open emotionally and loves analysing people and relationships, and I'm with her on that. We also have moments where her incessant demands for lifts and money thrust me to the edges of despair. I suppose all I'm doing here is defining life with a teenage girl.

What's been a constant, ever since she was very young, is a feeling that she is in some way an old soul, unafraid of the dark side of life. As a toddler this manifested itself in a startlingly deep voice, an oddly distant stare upon occasion and intense relationships with imaginary friends who often ended up dying in bizarre circumstances: 'Snowy's had an accident.' Now she's a teenager who likes nothing better than to cuddle up in bed and watch teenage vampires or, failing that, a crime documentary. Even though I'm reluctant to scratch the itch, she loves to dig away at my childhood, unearth details, talk about its effects.

As we wait for the lights, she suddenly whisks around.

'So *are* you happier?' she asks. 'Like the title of your book says, has the marathon really made you happy?'

'Well, it has a bit. Obviously, you know, I still get moody from time to time. I'm still, you know, Dad.'

'Yes. I've noticed that.'

'But there is a difference. When I think about my life, the stuff that happened when I was young—'

'Yes...?' Her eyes piqued in anticipation.

'There's a feeling of acceptance. I know it sounds bizarre, but something did change for me when I ran. It's weird. I'm not carrying it with me anymore. There's a peace there, it's finished.'

'And will you run more? Does it stop?'

'No. I'll always run. But it's not about time now. It's more about adventures, experience, long runs through deserts and jungles. If anything, I reckon it'll get intense in a different way, but all *that* stuff is over now. We really don't need to talk about it much.'

For some reason I thought she might be disappointed at this, but she wasn't, not at all. Her face immediately brightened, then she said something that only cemented her old soul reputation. 'It's like a fairy tale and she was the wicked witch. Since you ran the marathon, she's gone.'

And with that, the lights changed and she crossed the road. After gathering myself for a moment, I followed her down the hill.

We were going to the supermarket.

Acknowledgements

Before I wrote a book I always fantasised about the acknowledgement section. What a great thing to be able to do, to thank the people who have helped. Too numerous to mention but I'll give it a go. So thanks to…

Matt Gilbert, who gave me my first column at *Runner's World*, an essential part of my running resurrection. Then, of course, the team at *Runner's World* – Andy Dixon, Kerry McCarthy and Joe Mackie. Apologies for the consistently late submissions.

George Eden, my first coach, for the inspiration. The miles we shared! In my heart, literally.

The clubs I've run for: Scarborough Harriers, Thirsk and Sowerby, Richmond and Zetland, and latterly to all the London Heathsiders who inspired me so much during the period of this book. All members but specifically – Sarah Swinhoe, Dominic Jackson, Gavin Evans, Daniel Johns, Mario Cadete, Chris Hartley, Rob Shulman, Hoggy, Edward Adams, Richard Hewett. They were just going about their normal business that winter, but little did they know how important they were – HEATHSIDERS!

It's worth noting that since the sub-3 marathon, normal service has been resumed with Dominic. He soundly thrashes me over every surface and distance. Also in dispatches, Gavin recently ran a 2:52 marathon at the age of 59, in the process of winning an England vest! Hoggy was last seen scuttling around a training camp in Ethiopia.

Roisin Conaty – thanks for the inspiration. It would be remiss of me not to mention that this was the year Roisin wrote and starred in the brilliant Channel 4 sitcom *Gameface*, which I urge you to watch. So, despite the odd fall from grace, she had a far more productive year than I did.

Nick Walters, my man at David Luxton's, who encouraged me to dig deeper while writing the book and also gave me a lesson in how to write a decent synopsis.

The champion team at Bloomsbury. Matt Lowing – who gave me the initial 'Yes' and offered invaluable support and expertise at key moments during the process, always cheerfully expressed. Copy editor – Caroline Curtis – thank you, I wish I had you on my shoulder at all times when writing and to Sarah Skipper for all her help gathering the photos.

To my podcast partner, Robert Deering, without whom quite simply this book wouldn't have happened. It was he who showed me the way back to regular running – all those Mondays when I'd meet you hungover on the parkland walk. So much has changed! Let us have many more running adventures.

To the funniest unknown (but not for long) comedian in the world, Nick Dixon, currently smashing a comedy club near you. Thanks for having a look at the initial synopsis and pointing out it was Jeff Goldblum who'd forgotten his mantra. I hope one day you can forgive me for this oversight.

To Helen Ryan and Carrie Longton, thanks so much for reading the book in the early stages and providing valuable feedback and encouragement.

To my dear friend 'The Mac', who, though I support him onstage, gives me more support offstage than perhaps he imagines, 'Hello mate'.

To Dad, with love always. I didn't get time to talk about all the running we did together in and around Scarborough. I remain inspired by your performance in the Harrogate 16-mile road race circa 1985.

To my family – George, Bonita, Rudy. The dogs, Calypso and Billie Jean, and of course, last but not least, dearest Rachel. Thanks for the love and laughs. You couldn't possibly understand how happy and lucky I feel to walk among you in that noisy house on the hill. (If I could urge you all one last time – stop slamming the door. If everyone keeps slamming the door the lock will break again.)

In memoriam. Dashy, Tiger and Angelo. Gone, but not forgotten.

And finally to all the runners I've met or come into contact with over the years through the podcast Running Commentary or the column in *Runner's World*. Thanks so much for the inspiration. Good luck in all running endeavours. Enjoy every step.

Hopefully we'll meet in person, perhaps in a race over trail, roads or cross-country. I wish you all the best but be aware, if we're still together and its 200m from the finish – I will be trying to beat you.

So, let's sprint.